DDD17 (TRANSCRIBED) (TRANSLA

Winter 2008

WELCOME
!!TO-NIGHT · ONLY!!
A GREAT SPECTRAL AND METEORIC WONDER & NEVER BEFORE SEEN
IGGY FATUSE
WILL MAKE A RADIANT APPEARANCE!
THIS EXPLOSIVE BEAUTY,
— "THE HUMAN FIREFLY" —
Bound By Neither LAWS OF GRAVITY nor PRINCIPLES OF THERMOPHOTONICS
RIGHT BEFORE YOUR VERY EYES
WILL TRANSFORM
RANDOM ENERGY into VISIBLE LIGHT
TO RENDER HERSELF AT ONCE
WEIGHTLESS and LUMINOUS.
NO ORDINARY ACT OF SPONTANEOUS COMBUSTION!
NO SIMPLE FEAT OF LEVITATIONAL METAMORPHOSIS!
NO MERE TEMPERATURE-GRADIENT INVERSION MIRAGE!
In a Brilliant Aura of Sublime Courage — WITH NO EXTERNAL SOURCE OF IGNITION — This Daring Maverick
WILL ELEVATE TO AN EMINENCE
UPWARDS OF
FORTY-FOUR FEET
8 X THE HEIGHT OF THIS POSTER!!
before disappearing into a glowing streak in the sky.

WINTER 2008. THE EMBANKMENT, LONDON. THURSDAY OCTOBER 29, 7PM.

EXT. A BUILDING THAT LOOKS LIKE A DRAWING. THE CAPITAL'S FIRST OCTOBER
SNOW IN 80 YEARS,

INT. A DARK, SPOTLIT INTERIOR ORIENTED TO THE NORTH. ALONG THE WEST WALL
A ROW OF 5 VICTORIAN PRINTS ('REMARKABLE'). ALONG THE EAST WALL A FOLDED
PAPER PHOTOGRAM ('BESHTY'S POSSIBLE TRIANGLE'). IN THE CORNER OF THE
CEILING WHERE THE NORTH AND EAST WALLS MEET, A PORTRAIT ('GENESIS BREYER
P-ORRIDGE') ANGLED DOWN TOWARDS THE AUDIENCE, WHO NOW FILE IN. TERRY
RILEY'S 'IN C' IS BARELY AUDIBLE ABOVE THE GENERAL YAMMER.

etc.

D AND S APPROACH A PAIR OF ASYMMETRIC LECTERNS FROM OPPOSITE SIDES OF
THE ROOM. S CLEARS HIS THROAT. THE MUSIC FADES OUT TO SILENCE. THEY BEGIN
TO SPEAK SIMULTANEOUSLY, CHANNELED SEPARATELY THROUGH CORRESPONDING
LEFT AND RIGHT SPEAKERS.

S: Good evening, thanks to Somerset House for hosting us, and if you haven't done so already, please turn off your phones for the rest of the evening. Perhaps the best way to anticipate some of the themes that will recur between now and Friday night is to suggest some possible subtitles. I'm going to propose three, in slight homage to the Penrose Triangle—also known as the Impossible Triangle—printed in green over there to your right, my left [points], on top of the folded paper photogram by Walead Beshty, one of DOT DOT DOT 17's two front covers.

The first subtitle is VERFREMDUNGS-EFFEKT, VARIOUSLY TRANSLATED. This came up in conversation with Jennifer Higgie as she explained the nature of her play-in-progress, 'Carnival Theory', which she'll read from tomorrow. The term 'Verfremdungseffekt' was coined by Bertolt Brecht, and is basically a contraction of his breaking the 'fourth wall' —the final barrier between audience and actors. His intention was to prevent the viewer from slipping into passivity by making them fully

D: Good evening, welcome and thanks for coming. Over the next three evenings here we'll be presenting around ten talks of approximately 45 minutes each, with ten minute intermissions in between and a cheap bar at the back of the room over there [points]. Perhaps the best way to describe what we're intending with this set of talks is to briefly recount what we did for the first two versions of this group exhibition, 'Wouldn't It Be Nice ...', and to make it clear how they relate to the third incarnation here at the Embankment Galleries in Somerset House.

The first version of this exhibition was installed at the Centre d'Art Contemporain in Geneva almost a year ago to the day. For two and a half weeks during last October and November, we gathered together all of the contributors to DOT DOT DOT 15, including the printers and their stencil printing machines, in order to write, edit, design and print 3000 copies of the publication on location—literally in the space of the exhibition which contained it. On the penultimate day of the show, completed copies

3

aware of the conceits and devices of the theatre before them. And while it's no great leap to see how this approach informs DOT DOT DOT in general—and this issue in particular—what really attracted us to 'Verfremdungseffekt' was the fact that Jennifer had included not one but four common ways of translating the term into English: 'Alienation effect', 'Defamiliarization effect', 'Distancing effect', and 'Estrangement effect'. Jennifer admitted she'd drawn these definitions from Brecht's Wikipedia page. As you probably know, Wikipedia employs a process of 'Disambiguation' to distinguish between different references of the same term. This four-fold definition is, contrarily, an appropriate case of 'Ambiguation' instead.

The second subtitle is THE ALPHABET AS WORKING CLASS HIEROGLYPHICS. This was an offhand remark made by David the other week, which caused me to mentally double-take. He meant class in an entirely straightforward social sense, relating how the sheer quantity of symbols in the complex hieroglyphic system meant only the very rich could afford the time and materials to learn it, as opposed to the modular alphabet which, having just over twenty characters, was much more accessible and therefore democratic. As it turned out, I'd completely misunderstood. I thought he was talking about a kind of class system WITHIN graphic languages, in which hieroglyphics were a primary class, being closer to the source of the things the symbols represented, and the alphabet a secondary class, being further away, or more abstracted. The analogy to DOT DOT DOT 17 is that these evenings ought to be considered the primary source, and in some sense symbolic, and the eventual printed publication a distinctly secondary form, and more literal.

The third subtitle is ISOMORPHISM, BORROWED FROM MATHEMATICS. This is a term which, for our purposes, can be defined as the translation from one form to another with no information lost in the process. It might, however, be refracted. A pole poked into water and just a little off and just taking a little bit longer in the manner of all things refracted. The last line was a quote from David Foster Wallace's novel 'Infinite Jest', but isomorphism was initially articulated to us through a mathematically-minded designer working in the middle of the last century, Anthony Froshaug, who, for reasons that overlap with those above, named his first company Isomorph. He also once defined the process of design as translating a problem, set of problems, from one language, one set of symbols, to another, with love.

of the issue finally arrived back from the binders to the gallery space, where they were then displayed on a bookshelf on the floor for a single day. When the show travelled to Zurich some months later, we simply exhibited this same bookshelf of completed issues on a wall, together with five framed pieces of the original source material behind the issue's images, also more or less produced on site in Geneva. For the next and probably last version here at Somerset House, then, we wanted to do something less ambitious than the complete production setup in Geneva and more ambitious than the detached display in Zurich.

Financially speaking, the only way to continue producing DOT DOT DOT at the moment is to use invitations such as these pragmatically, in order to both facilitate and inform production. So when we were originally asked to participate in Geneva we proposed that we use their particular resources—their considerable funding, staff and space—to direct the next issue. And when invited to contribute something equally substantial here in London, we proposed much the same idea, though now specific to the particularities of Somerset House. This led us to stage a series of talks as raw material, essentially performing the texts that will comprise DOT DOT DOT 17 with a bunch of mostly London-based contributors in order to minimize travel and accommodation costs. As usual, each piece should be at once ABOUT and AN EMBODIMENT OF its subject, and together ought to congeal into some kind of overarching theme. Each of the talks, then, will attempt a different form of delivery, from the entirely improvised to the entirely scripted, after which we'll attempt to translate each one —through ink on paper—accordingly.

Last week at an art school we were asked whether projects like these necessarily adhere to the old Modernist maxim of absolute commitment to truth in materials, transparency of form, etcetera etcetera ... and the only answer we could reasonably offer was an apparent contradiction, or paradox. While we're certainly concerned with the ideas and ideals of such so-called "truth", we're equally disinterested in absolutes, doctrines and dogmas—an answer which effectively cancels itself out with the ill-logic of the classic self-detonating sentence, "This statement is false." Another trite example is, "The first rule is: there are no rules." The first rule here, then is that absolutely everything that will constitute DOT DOT DOT 17 must be spoken or shown in this room over the course of the next three evenings—which is impossible.

4

Which usefully brings us to our first speaker, Richard Hollis, who met Froshaug at Ulm in 1960 and shared classes with him at the Central School here in London in the early 1970s. He once told me that when Froshaug was teaching, Richard would often be drafted in from the corridor to translate Froshaug's ideas—from English to English—into accessible language. So, Richard …

THE RIGHT LECTERN IS REMOVED AS RICHARD HOLLIS APPEARS WITH A CHAIR AND POSITIONS IT IN FRONT OF A SCREEN ONTO WHICH THE FOLLOWING IMAGES ARE PROJECTED IN SEQUENCE. HE BEGINS A RUNNING COMMENTARY IMPROVISED FROM THESE NOTES, POINTING OUT DETAILS WITH A STICK AND MAKING OCCASIONAL NON-VERBAL SOUNDS (SCREAMS, GUNFIRE ETC.),

If we had to choose between losing our hearing or our sight, most people would choose to lose sound (the ear) rather than vision (the eye). I'm going to talk about how we convey the idea of sound—most often the voice—in a silent world, almost as if we were deaf. What I'm going to say is really a commentary on the images rather than the images being illustrations of an argument or theory.

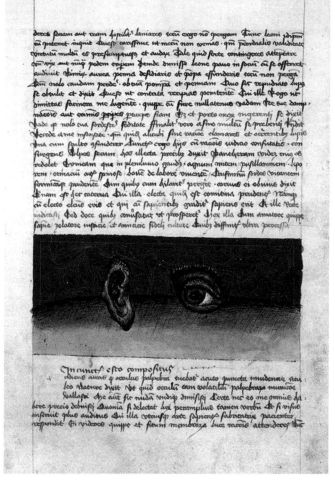

1. This image from the Middle Ages shows the primary importance attributed to the ear (aural/acoustic) and the eye (optical/visual) at the time. They were considered the means by which we come to understand the world. Writing & reading are to do with the eye: they are visual & optical. Listening & speaking are to do with the ear (and the mouth): they are aural & acoustic.

2. With the eyes, without language, we can understand a great deal—from gesture.

3. For the deaf, gesture is crucial.

aap	roos	zeef	muur	voet	neus
lam	gijs	riem	muis	ei	juk
jet	wip	does	hok	bòk	kous

```
        Writing        Listening


        Reading        Speaking
```

6. This Dutch school textbook (not for the deaf) shows that phonetic alphabet sounds are made of combinations of letters and depend on context. The vowel sounds are in a different colour. Eye and ear have an equal role.

7. L is for Language. Writing & reading are to do with the eye: they are visual & optical. Listening & speaking are to do with the ear (and the mouth): they are aural & acoustic.

sound¹ (saund) n. **1. a.** a periodic disturbance in tl density of a fluid or in the elastic strain of a solid, vibrating object. It has a velocity in air at sea leve metres per second (743 miles per hour) and travels waves. **b.** (*as modifier*): *a sound wave*. **2.** (*modifier*) o radio as distinguished from television: *sound broad radio*. **3.** the sensation produced by such a periodic the organs of hearing. **4.** anything that can be particular instance, quality, or type of sound: *the so water*. **6.** volume or quality of sound: *a radio with* ɪ the area or distance over which something can be he *within the sound of Big Ben*. **8.** the impression or something: *I don't like the sound of that*. **9.** *Phonetic* effect produced by a specific articulation or set of rɛ tions. **10.** (*often pl.*) *Slang*. music, esp. rock, jazz, or ɪ report, news, or information, as about a person, event to cause (something, such as an instrument) to make an instrument, etc.) to emit a sound. **13.** to an announced by a sound: *to sound the alarm*. **14.** (*intr.*) be heard. **15.** (*intr.*) to resonate with a certain quali *to sound loud*. **16.** (*copula*) to give the impressio

10. A single word is not simple. In this dictionary entry, 'sound' has many meanings, even if the sound of the word is the same: 1. what is heard (16 variations of meaning); 2. undamaged, solid (12); 3. measure of depth (5); 4. narrow strait of water (3), eg. Plymouth Sound.

6

ā	à	á	ā̄	å̄			ȧ
ē	è	ê̇	e	e	ê	é	ě		è
ī							
y							
o					ó	ȯ	*
u							
th	th	ch	tu	ti
sh	ch	sc	s	g
c	t	si	z	
s	d	f	q	q
s	x	gh	ph	qu

11. We think there are 5 vowels in English, but there are actually 21 vowel sounds. Consonants have their own variations, eg. 'T' can make the same sound as 'SH' or 'S' (nation, shine, sugar).

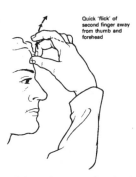

Quick 'flick' of second finger away from thumb and forehead

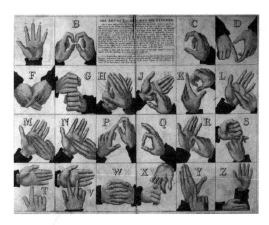

4. The successful sign language for the deaf was established by the early 19th century. It had won the battle over alphabetic signs.

5. Plainly for the deaf, alphabetic language was too slow, despite being connected with the alphabet through being printed.

ABCDEFGHIJKLMNOPQRSTUVWXYZ
abcdefghijklmnopqrstuvwxyz
.,:;'…!?¡¿1234567890£$¥@®©™%‰#§
Æ OE æ œ ß fi fl & ƒ ¶ ¬ ^ † ‡   µ
Ä Á À Â Ã Å Ç É Ë È Ê Ï Í Ì Î Ñ Ö Ó Ò Ô Õ Ø Ü Ú Ù Ÿ
ä á à â ã å ç ë é è ê ï í ì î ñ ó ò ô õ ø ü ú ù û ÿ ª º
+ ± ÷ - = ≠ ~ _ - — < >
/ | \ ( ) [ ] { } ‹ › « » ' ' " " * • · ¹ ° ⁄ ∕ ⌐ ¬ – ‿ ˘ ∘   ˝ ˇ
Roman   ˌ ˎ

8. All we have to convey sounds of language (at least in much of the world) are the 26 signs, plus numerals and punctuation.

9. In our culture we have decided to organise the alphabet into letters/words/sentences/paragraphs/columns/pages in a sequence in a horizontal/vertical (orthogonal) arrangement.

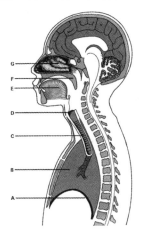

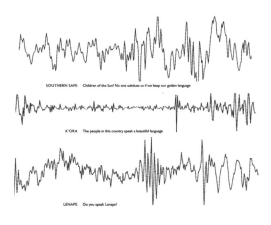

SOUTHERN SAMI   Children of the Sun! No one subdues us if we keep our golden language

K'ORA   The people in this country speak a beautiful language

LENAPE   Do you speak Lenape?

12. The human production of sound is physiologically complex. Given our varied build it's not surprising that our individual voices are distinct and identifiable.

7

13. The sound waves of 3 different tribes. Although the messages are different, so are their relative rhythm and pitch.

Thy drugs are quick. Thus with a kiss I die.   *He falls*
Enter Friar Laurence, with lantern, crow, and spade

FRIAR
Saint Francis be my speed! How oft tonight
Have my old feet stumbled at graves! Who's there?

BALTHASAR
Here's one, a friend, and one that knows you well.

FRIAR
Bliss be upon you! Tell me, good my friend,
What torch is yond that vainly lends his light
To grubs and eyeless skulls? As I discern,
It burneth in the Capels' monument.

BALTHASAR
It doth so, holy sir; and there's my master,
One that you love.

14. The simple typesetting of a play. Difficult to read without assuming the voice of the character in one's head. The placing of some responses also helps the rhythm—the interplay of two actors.

15. This 18th-century attempt at recording the voice uses a kind of musical notation. With it you can recreate the intonation of an actor's voice.

18. Over the last century, artists & designers have tried to suggest sound by breaking the horizontal/vertical layout of words. This is a representation of scattered 'peanuts' by Germano Facetti.

19. The Futurists attempted to describe sound (& often noise) on paper. This is Marinetti's representation of the War: 'After the Battle of the Marne General Joffre visits the front'. It includes loving endearments and patriotic slogans alongside the noise of guns.

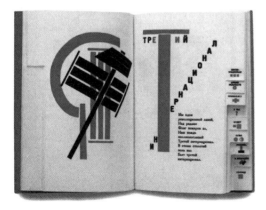

22. El Lissitzky's famous book 'For Reading Out Loud' did not, in fact, convey sound typographically.

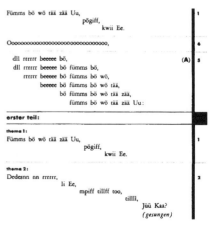

23. Unlike Lissitzky, Jan Tschichold laid out Kurt Schwitters' famous phonetic 'Ursonate' exactly as Schwitters performed it—like a musical score.

16. Skipping two centuries. After radio and with the arrival of TV and commercials, printed advertising tried to extend the spoken langauge of voiceovers onto the printed page.

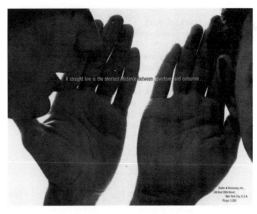

17. And printed advertising used the image of the speaker and listener to make a point: an advertising agency's appeal to clients.

20. While Gino Severini showed the noise (and coloured light) of the Conga being danced.

21. The Dadaists also tried to imply tone of voice, but using various typefaces in the conventional orthogonal format dictated by the rectangular base of letters of metal type locked in a rectangular frame. This is by Hugo Ball: a sound poem without meaning.

24. Double-page spread from an illustrated version of a play by Ionesco. Design by Massin. The type was printed letterpress on condoms, stretched, and reproduced photographically.

25. The opening of a French edition of Mark Twain's 'Tom Sawyer', designed by Pierre Faucheux. The exclamation mark is part of the original text.

9

26. Faucheux also made an exhibiton for French radio
—but without sound.

27. Asked to vote in a referendum to approve the
European Union treaty, the French did so … just!

stille
stille

stille die
stille

die stille
stillen

stiele

die stiele
der stille

die stiele
der stille
stillen
die stille

stille

stille

do you think design should be impersonal ?

        Yes I do really   hm its
the ident its not the **designers** personality that should be evident   its the
personality of the em of the subject matter which I think should be
significant *Because I think it's terrible when designers have style*
    I mean   unless its completely *bland*   like not with the advantage of That
was the idea of the Swiss style that they wanted to have something that was
totally international what did they call this , *super national anonymous format* which erm
because they thought that words just   put across meaning and
if you used like **type** and so on you were giving an inflection an accent
giving a tendency to the meaning which was not what was intended by
the linguistic meaning.

30. Concrete poetry utilises space and the dispositon
of words—here to suggest silence, or quiet ('Stille'
in German) and 'Stiele' (the stalk of a plant). The
similarity of the words' sound is the basis of the poem.

31. A straightforward attempt by a student to
transcribe an interview with me. Typeset to give
a sense of the speed, hesitation and emphasis of
my speech.

34. From Wassily Kandinsky's 'Sounds' ('Klänge').
By chance, the first line of 'Spring' is "Shut up."

35. The usual way of representing sound in graphics.

David Hockney: een interview

interviewer: Mark Glazebrook

B. Ik kan me herinneren dat in het begin
n de jaren zestig het woord literair op de academies
n slechte klank had. Ondanks de verwantschap
een surrealisme en abstract expressionisme werd
raire schilderkunst in het heiligdom van de
hodoxe moderne kunst beschouwd als ketterij.
b je ooit scrupules gehad ten aanzien van je
niskenbaar literaire bronnen... Blake,
iltman, Cavafy, de gebroeders Grimm, of ten
izien van je vroegere neiging om verhalend te
ilderen?

D.H. Nee, eigenlijk niet, dat wil zeggen het is op dat
moment nooit een probleem voor mij geweest. Wat mijn etsen
betreft, daar deed zich dit probleem niet voor, omdat ik daarbij
lijnen gebruik en ik vind dat een lijn op de een of andere
manier een eigen verhaal vertelt. De etsen zijn dus nog literair
in die zin, dat zij inderdaad iets te vertellen hebben, terwijl
mijn schilderijen hun literair karakter verloren ongeveer toen
ik naar Californië vertrok in 1964. Ik geloof niet, dat ik daarna
nog de literatuur als bron voor het schilderen gebruikt heb,
terwijl ik vóór die tijd een aantal schilderijen gemaakt heb naar
poëzie van... Whitman, Auden, Blake en Cavafy.

Wat vormde voor jou de grootste
itrekkingskracht in de poëzie van Cavafy?
idat ze met kunst te maken hebben? of om hun
snheid ten aanzien van problemen als liefde,
isualiteit, of...

About two years after completing this painting Hockney referred to it in connection with his **Second Marriage** painting:

"I decided to use a device that I'd used before (in the Tea Painting – shown at the Young Contemporaries in February 1962 – with a figure in an illusionistic style) and build up a sort of isometric projection of a cube (a room) to place my figures in."

Cambridge Opinion 37, 1963

In 1964, David Sylvester referred as follows to this painting, having listed the artists by whom he thought Pop Art ought to be judged: "I have excluded David Hockney because he's not a Pop artist, though usually called one –

28. The convention of the interview: different speaker, different position in space, different font.

29. Catalogue editor: light Egyptian slab-serif type. Artist: light Grotesque type within bold quote marks.

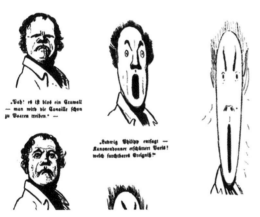

32. The diplomatic faces of the revolutionary year 1848. The expressions suggest tone of voice.

33. Speech bubbles have a long history.

36. Comics relate both sound effects and speech.

37. And in a narrative strip noise can be represented phonetically. Incidentally, the direction of reading here is ambiguous.

38. The same means using bold in the bubbles and phonetics for the sound effects—the larger the louder. Detail of a strip in the Guardian by Posy Simmonds, 1987.

39. Typeset narrative, lettered speech and bold emphasis. The large, bold, dropped-capital initial letters help navigate the reader's eye. From Posy Simmonds, 'Gemma Bovery', 1999.

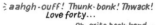

40. Sounds are crucial here. A woman watching tennis on TV instead of working at her computer while her husband takes the children out so she can get on with her work.

The sounds are (from the TV)
: the players grunting
: the sound of the ball being hit
: the umpire's voice
: the Australian commentator
: the plummy tones of the English commentator
—and other sounds in the home.
Dotted lines indicate the source of the sound.
From Posy Simmonds, 'Literary Life', 2002.

13

41. A montage by John Heartfield, 'Berlin Dialect', ie. speaking out of one's arse.

42. The phonetic "NOOOO" is not truly successful here as it represents the wrong sound. But the face does the work.

45. Again, context is everything.

46. The Soviets regularly used image to conjure voice. In our culture, at least, the gesture here is unclear: is the sailor whistling or whispering?

49. A Morse Code 'V'.

50. Musical notation from medieval graffito in an English church.

43. The face again. Something is happening. But what? A scream?

44. In pain?

47. The V-sign: V for Victory, Victoire, Vrijheid, Vittoria; English, French, Dutch, Italian.

48. The first few bars of Beethoven's Vth Symphony. Music turned into image. The notes make up the beat of the Morse code for 'V': dot dot dot dash.

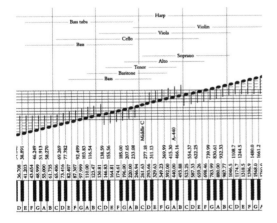

51. The tonal range of the piano at bottom compared with instruments of the orchestra above.

15

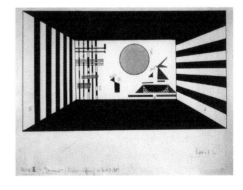

52. Kandinsky's supposedly musical design of a setting for Modest Mussorgsky's piano suite 'Pictures at an Exhibition'.

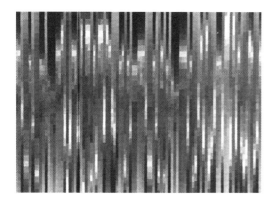

53. Music as the basis of visual art: Swiss artist Jakob Weder has used Bach.

54. Another Swiss painter, Richard Paul Lohse, played scales with colour. The word 'harmony' in relation to colour demonstrates common aesthetic notions in aural and visual art.

MATRIMONIAL HARMONICS.

57. Same again: piano, singing, baby, cat, canary, the caged birds at the hamster's feet ... deafening.

58. Deafening, or potentially deafening.

61. The interaction of an image with the imagined sound of a Beatles lyric.

62. 'Germany First!', designed by John Heartfield, about the 'haves' & 'have-nots'. Word & image again. Made for reading slowly. Every sentence a new line, but broken so that the image qualifies the words, like an adjective, but with at least one meaning.

55. Rudolph de Harak's suggestion of an Alpenhorn and the sound over the mountains is conveyed here with real economy.

56. Reactions to sound are an obvious way of showing its existence.

60. Hans-Rudolf Lutz's demonstration of a newspaper's reliance on image (right) which carries the message immediately before they are given a context by text (left).

59. The CIA's efforts to explode Castro with his cigar.

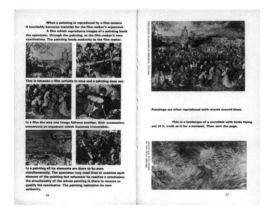

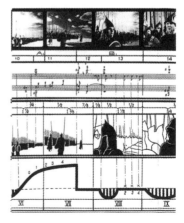

63. 'Ways of Seeing', a book version of four TV programmes. Notably a presentation of images without music, now an essential aspect of TV presentations of art.

64. Finally, the film director Sergei Eisenstein used diagrams as illustrations. Here the frames of a film are linked to the score in line 2; positioning & tonal weight in line 3; the relation of tone & movement in line 4.

APPLAUSE. RETURNING TO THE RIGHT LECTERN, S ANNOUNCES THE DRILL FOR THE NEXT 3 EVENINGS: EACH TALK WILL BE PUNCTUATED BY A 10 MIN. BREAK FOR DRINKING AND SMOKING.

ON REASSEMBLING, D INTRODUCES JAMES GOGGIN WHO IN TURN INTRODUCES HIS SUPPORTING CAST OF MARIA FUSCO, WILL HOLDER, RICHARD HOLLIS AND MAKI SUZUKI, THEN DESCRIBES THE REASONS BEHIND THE QUESTION HE INTENDS TO ASK THEM: HOW DO YOU READ IN LONDON IN 2008?*

J : Interactive art, especially in its high-tech, fetishist variety, can frequently leave you feeling more intellectually and emotionally passive than much supposedly autonomous work. Often you feel treated like a chimpanzee, encouraged to perform menial tasks to reach the banana. If 'interactivity' leaves you cold, perhaps you will empathise with its neglected sibling: what the Austrian Philosopher Robert Pfaller has termed 'interpassivity'.

Pfaller's notion was originally inspired by Slavoj Žižek's observation that the canned laughter of sitcoms doesn't so much trigger our own laughter as substitute for it. Exhausted after a hard day's work, it is as if we delegate even the passive enjoyment of laughing. But the prime example of interpassivity is the way many people use their video to record more films than they could ever watch. Strangely, this doesn't necessarily leave you unsatisfied: whether the tapes are neatly sorted on your shelves or piled up, unlabelled, beside the TV, you can enjoy a sense of relief that you didn't miss a particular art-house film or a certain documentary. While you were working into the small hours, the VHS watched the film for you: you delegated the enjoyment and edification to the video recorder in order to be able to remain active.

The computer, combining production and consumption under one roof, is, of course, the perfect medium of interpassivity: while you write that important text, in the background it sorts myriad newsgroup messages you will never read into compartmentalised mailboxes; downloads software you will never use; and stores pictures from your digital camera which you will never look at. Of course, you could if you wanted to. The shy boy-next-door in 'American Beauty' (1999), Ricky Fitts (Wes Bentley), uses his camcorder to filter the world: it enables him to be a functional member of society while recording hundreds of hours of 'everyday beauty'—more than he could ever watch. He conceals his dope-dealing from his Nazi memorabilia-collecting father by hiding his stash behind the video cassettes. This is an allegory of interpassivity, a quotidian cross

between fetishism and compulsive behaviour: your active working life is a cover-up for your 'true' passive desires that reside in the machines and objects which process information you hardly use.

Interpassivity is usually, but not always, a facet of collecting. This is exemplified in a slightly uncanny story I heard recently. For some time, a friend's father had been enthusiastically filming his grandson with a new video camera, but it turned out that he had never changed the tape, thus erasing every single hour he had recorded with the following one. The father, technically naïve, claimed he thought that the tape could somehow store all those hours and hours of filming. But it dawned on my friend that his father had never really intended to keep the footage he had shot—as if it were meant only to be recorded but never watched. The interpassive desire was to take part in family life without having to show affection, using the camera as a shield and recording as an excuse, as if his real desire was to eliminate these 'memorable' moments.

"People take pictures of each other just to prove that they really existed", the Kinks sang in 1968. And if that was the Existentialist age of interpassivity, we have now reached the virtual: interpassive people don't have to read, watch or listen to the information proving someone or something exists—they just need to know that information about that existence exists. You could update the Marxist notion of commodity fetishism and say that interpassivity is information fetishism: you don't know whether you'll ever use it, but enjoy having it anyway. In the old days, a copy of Proust's 'In Search of Lost Time' sitting on the shelf suggested that someday, when you had three weeks with time and energy to spare, you could read the entire thing in one go. In the future, when every book is instantly available on the Net, zillions of texts will be downloaded and stored, but not read. The entry on your credit card statement will be the reward, an indication that you have done something 'cultural'.

In the 19th century, the wealthy bourgeois

18

developed an art form out of squandering their time; nowadays, if you're older than a student and younger than a pensioner, you simply have to be seen reading a book. Interpassivity is the ultimate quirk of the upwardly mobile petit-bourgeois, compensation for the guilt of not being an appreciative connoisseur, not being educated, and not being politically aware (how many thick books and drawn-out films, from 'Das Kapital' to Claude Lanzmann's 'Shoah', are bought but never entirely read or watched?). What else is the average book shelf than a monument to the interpassivity of the educated classes?

Viennese artist Julius Deutschbauer didn't have much trouble finding enough people to contribute books to his 'Bibliothek Ungelesener Bücher' ('Library of Unread Books', 1997–present); it includes everything from Stalin to Derrida to Allen Carr's 'The Easy Way To Stop Smoking'. Deutschbauer shows that what appears to be the pitiful residue of engagement is so much better than the pseudo-enlightened cynicism of CEOs or politicians boasting that they are just too busy to read. Interpassivity stems from the contradictions of an economy which demands that people always be sociable and functional in a team, while still maintaining a perceptive, introspective, creative side. As interpassivity serves to simulate the latter, it may keep the economy running—barely. But it also contains the potential to turn the tables: the information is there, and, one day, you could stop industriously filing it and start to actually use it. You could—if you really wanted to. ∎

* What happened next is represented here not by direct transcription, but by the text that inspired it, Jörg Heiser's 'Lazy Days'—an article within an article which necessitates a footnote within a footnote. James …
"My phantom piece on HOW TO READ is rapidly turning into HOW TO WRITE. In fact,

I've discovered something I probably knew all along—and which came up in the discussion with Maria, Will, Richard, and Maki—that the best way to suddenly find more time to read is by attempting to write something.

For some time I've been contemplating the act of reading and how to do it. In terms of interpretation, reference and comprehension, but also on a very practical level: how do we find the time to read, and where and when do we do it? For me the question has pretty much dictated a system where I no longer cycle to get around London, but instead deliberately take slow buses in order to have reading time.

I often see my practice as ostensibly working to pay the bills for my family and endeavouring to live in London while striving to retain a critical approach to my work. This includes reading and writing, of course —but invariably at 3 o'clock in the morning. I'm curious to ask other people very basic questions about how, when and where they read and how it affects what and how they read it.

So I finally pulled all my boxes of old Frieze magazines down from the shelf in an attempt to dig out the article I once mentioned to you, in which Jörg Heiser explores Slavoj Žižek's notion of 'interpassivity': the contemporary condition where collecting/recording/consuming increasingly acts as a proxy for actual viewing/listening/reading. I spent quite some time flicking through many issues looking for the piece, then eventually stopped and thought, wait a minute, Frieze MUST have put some of their old articles online by now—and so they had. One minute later a search for 'Jörg Heiser' pulled up 'Lazy Days' from issue 56, January–February 2001 … the very issue I had in my hands ready to flick through before I gave up and went online.

In a way this is a perfect illustration of what I think is my point, or one of them: that reading something already requires or presupposes the reading of something else through assumptions and references made by the writer (re: any issue of DDD). As such, the introduction to my piece should be me briefly describing this, then simply directing the reader to read Heiser's article in full. An article within an article, with a footnote which supplants and takes over my 'real' text (re: Maria Fusco's reading re: Flann O'Brien's 'The Third Policeman').
Perhaps this is just my interpassive way of getting the piece written at all."

MORE APPLAUSE HERALDS A SECOND BREAK, DURING WHICH 2 TRAVEL POSTERS ARE PROJECTED ONTO THE SCREEN. THE AUDIENCE EVENTUALLY GATHERS ITSELF AND SETTLES AS S BEGINS TO SPEAK FROM THE LEFT LECTERN.

S : The genesis of the next piece is the work of Falke Pisano, an artist whose absence tonight will hopefully be made conspicuous by Will Holder. For some time now we've been drawn to her graphic work[1] but put off by the language that surrounds it. This is extra-problematic inasmuch as the writing is clearly a symbiotic aspect of the work, not merely a supporting device. In other words, at least half the story. As it happens, Falke has been

collaborating on a book with Will towards resolving precisely this blockage, and so we invited them to talk about and around it here.

Unfortunately, Falke couldn't make it, but fortunately this embodies the issue: what happens when there's no-one around to stand up for—or to—the work. Will will speak of Falke's work from the left lectern, and of the poetics of concrete poetry which informs their collaboration, from the right lectern.

SKEGNESS

IS SO BRACING

Illustrated Guide from Secretary. Advancement Association,
Skegness, or any L·N·E·R Enquiry Office.

SKEGNESS

IS SO BRACING

Illustrated Guide from Secretary, Advancement Association,
Skegness, or any L·S·E·R Enquiry Office.

WILL HOLDER GLARES AT THE AUDIENCE, GRIPPING THE RIGHT LECTERN. DURING
THE PIECE HE RECITES DIRECTLY FROM SEVERAL IMAGES OF CONCRETE POETRY.
THE POSTERS REMAIN PROJECTED BEHIND AND ABOVE HIM THROUGHOUT AS HE
SHUTTLES BACK AND FORTH BETWEEN THE 2 LECTERNS.

W H :

Dear Stuart,

My own inability to speak in public without a script
has been demonstrated once more
at the joint F. R. DAVID/DOT DOT DOT book launch
at Castillo Corrales/Section 7 in Paris the other week,

and it seems that when the moment comes,

I become incapable of verbally paraphrasing
my editorial activities of the past 6 months.

(Obviously this handicap is my reason for being
so interested in speech-as-production, instructions,
plans and scripts:

my work becomes my own self-correcting course,
my ATTEMPT TO EVOLVE).

I often think of how calmly you can recount your tales—
or those of another—

from memory, though I also know that
neither of us is more or less sensitive
or aware when it comes to information.

And obviously this ties in to your Foster Wallace
as opposed to my Pynchon.[2]

People (documentation) behave differently
when you put a camera in their face,
or when you put them on stage.

This (feedbacked) discrepancy
between the document and the instruction
is what I'm interested in:

the potential of the reversal
of the perceived roles of the two,

ie. the presence of the recording (document)
as being instructional to that which is being recorded.

("esse est percepi")[3]

The main body of Falke Pisano's work contains accounts of transformations that take place in between language and objects. In later works this account could be seen as a speculative description of a future event that will construct an object, yet replace its actual presence. The event is something that happens to the object AND the event is an object in itself.

One of Ian Hamilton Finlay's recent works
is a screen-print entitled 'Homage to Gomringer'.

The heavy cruiser Prinz Eugen is sketched out
against the neutral grey background,
calling to mind the comparable profile
of a full-rigged ship in the screen-print's predecessor
'Homage to Mozart'.

Eugen Gomringer, progenitor of the European movement
of Concrete poetry,
is identified with the immaculate design
of the modern warship just as the strains of Mozart
could be identified with the billowing rococo forms
of the sailing ship.

But there is also an allegory underpinning
the use of Prinz Eugen at this juncture.

When its dedicated German crew handed over the warship
at the end of the Second World War,
ten out of eleven engines were working.

But by the time that the Americans had sailed
the Prinz Eugen to Honolulu,
only one of these was still in operation.

The same thing has happened,
Finlay implacably infers,
to the "Cruiser Concrete poetry".[4]

Critics have attempted to define concrete poetry,
place it in an international context,
discuss its historical influences,
isolate its typographical innovations,
and judge its impact on the world of art.
Yet very few have judged it as literature,
and no one has discussed in depth its contribution
to the genre it has been assigned: poetry.

One of the most important manifestations
of poetic style—metaphor—traditionally has been used

to establish a relationship between two things
by using a word or words figuratively
instead of literally.

Metaphor directs the reader to a sense
of the relationship—not to an exact term—
thereby allows the reader to supply an image
from his own experience.

In that way it transcends denotative meanings
inherent in any term
and allows the reader to supply the connotations
most immediate to him.

The twentieth century's obsession with the impotency
of its own verbal power
has inspired the poet to manipulate this metaphoric power
in new and different ways.

In the present century this linguistic technique must
communicate the figurative meaning by manipulating
the literal object and it must enrich the poetic structure
by demanding the reader's inference.

Of course metaphor has traditionally been used
in this way.

In addition to such standard usage however,
metaphor must now function as vital language once did,
and that is to present the literal images
and to serve as signs for the concrete 'things'
that words once symbolized.[5]

Eugen Gomringer, 'Silencio'

silencio silencio silencio
silencio silencio silencio
silencio   silencio
silencio silencio silencio
silencio silencio silencio[6]

The very letters of the poem itself serve
as the metaphoric vehicle for a tenor
that is nothing more than
perceiver participation in the language itself.

This personal response
is the only 'meaning' the concrete poem as metaphor has.
The perceiver must interact with the linguistic sign
(or signs)
on the page to form the meaning of the metaphor/poem.

The concrete poem is precisely that metaphor
with a concrete vehicle (the linguistic sign)
and a concrete tenor
(the perceivers'—poet's and reader's—response).

The perceiver moves from letters,
words, or phrases in an order
that in the end produces
the same total number of combinations
experienced by any other perceiver.[7]

Max Bense, 'Statistical Text'

es, ist, wenn, aber, doch, nicht; es ist, es doch,
es aber, wenn es, wenn ist, es nicht, aber ist, doch
ist, wenn doch, wenn aber, nicht ist, aber doch,
doch nicht, wenn nicht, aber nicht; wenn es ist,
es aber ist, ist es doch, wenn es aber, wenn es doch,
es aber doch, we nicht ist, es doch nicht, wenn doch
wenn es nicht, doch nicht ist, wenn aber doch, wenn
nicht ist, ist aber nicht, wenn doch nicht, wenn aber
nicht, aver doch nicht; wenn es aber ist, es aber
doch is, wenn es doch ist, wenn es aber doch, es
doch nicht ist, wenn es nicht ist, wenn aber nicht ist,
nicht, wenn es doch nicht, wenn doch nicht ist, aber
doch nicht ist, wenn aber nicht ist, wenn aber doch
nicht; wenn es doch nicht ist, wenn aber doch nicht ist,
wenn es aber doch nicht, wenn aber doch nicht ist;
wenn es aber doch nicht ist.[8]

The relationships between letters,
words,
or signs in the poem
and the senses that respond to them
are not inherent in the page:
the perceiver must forge the bond.

The concrete poem therefore requires
the perceiver's participation
to complete the poem/metaphor.[9]

In finding, selecting, and putting down these words
[the poet]
creates 'thought-objects'
and leaves the task of association to the reader,
who becomes a collaborator and,
in a sense,
the completer of the poem.[10]

This active participation is crucial
to the success of the poetic metaphor.[11]

Program: do it yourself
the reader (operator)
may go on at pleasure
doing new semantic variations
within the given parameter [12]

The poem ultimately means nothing
until the reader completes the vehicle
by participating in the exercise.

The sensorily perceivable metaphor
achieves literal reality in the concrete poems
that are nothing if not seen, spoken,
heard, and touched by reader participation.[13]

; and by using the reader's/perceiver's sensibility
to complete the 'meaning' of the metaphor
he facilitates reader contact
with the real world of the poem.[14]

The real world of the Poem,
to which the concrete poetry metaphor points,
is not located outside of the page it is printed on.[15]

This, of course, asks a great deal of the reader.
He must now perceive the poem as an object
and participate in the poet's act of creating it,
for the concrete poem communicates
first and foremost
its structure.

Those poets claimed that the concrete poem
"deals with a communication of forms,
of a structure-content,
not with the usual message communication."
It can be thought of as a kind of shorthand,
a telegraphic message,
for it aims at the least common multiple of language,
hence its tendency to
nounising and verbification.[16]

The arrangement of the characters
attempts to explore a non-linear method of reading,
breaking with the usual syntactic arrangement
of discrete units,
an analogy which could extend
to the re-arrangement of geographical,
social, mnemonic or conceptual relations.[17]

Augusto De Campos, 'Brazil'

here are the bare bodies
lovers kinless
brotherone, womoanother
meover, sheneath
sheechome
duplamlinfantonesever
seedintowomb
thisshe, thathe
inhumanother[18]

In defense of her work, Falke Pisano repeatedly insists
that the constructed object can only have one form,
which implies that this description of events can only
follow one course, and materialise in one way.

'Cannibal Manifesto'
by Oswaldro de Andrade

Only Cannibalism unites us. Socially. Economically.
Philosophically.
The unique law of the world. The disguised expression
of all individualisms, all collectivisms. Of all religions.
Of all peace treaties.

Tupi or not tupi that is the question.

Against all catechisms. And against the mother of
the Gracos.

I am only interested in what's not mine. The law of men.
The law of the cannibal.

What dominated over truth was clothing, an impermeable
layer between the interior world and the exterior world.
Reaction against people in clothes. The American cinema
will tell us about this.

Sons of the sun, mother of living creatures.
Fiercely met and loved, with all the hypocrisy of longing:
importation, exchange, and tourists. In the country
of the big snake.

It's because we never had grammatical structures or
collections of old vegetables. And we never knew
urban from suburban, frontier country from continental.
Lazy on the world map of Brazil.

One participating consciousness, one religious rhythm.
Against all the importers of canned conscience.

27

For the palpable existence of life. And let Levy-Bruhl
go study prelogical mentality.[19]

PRODUCING TRANSFORMATIONS: this formula permeated
the work of the Brazilian artists Hélio Oiticica and Lygia Clark.
It meant, in one aspect, that they engaged themselves radically
in their own lives, living a process of permanent actualization,
through self construction, deconstruction,
and experimentation. Unlike body-artists,
however, their main support was not their own bodies,
but those of the others: the pattern

YOU the spectator
ME the artist

was sensorially reversed by them into the conceptual flux

YOUwillbecoME

not through a simple mirror-like inversion, but in the
sense of moving YOU from the spectator's passive position
to the active and singular role of being the subject of your
own experience.[20]

Falke Pisano's work consists of the performative
act of writing instructions, which only become material
for the object under construction when they are
released from the confines of the printed page, through
reading.

In literary theory, description often has been considered
to be the handmaiden of narrative. Mieke Bal dismantles
this logocentric hierarchy between narrative and
description by arguing that every description is a narrative.
She prefers to approach signs of the real not by, assigning
them to a category, such as description, but as elements
within narration.[21]

Dear Pierre,

One of the cubists
—I forget who—
said it was after all difficult
for THEM to make cubism because
they did not have,
as we have,
the example of cubism to help them.

28

I wonder if we are not
all a little in the dark,
still
as to the real significance of 'concrete'
...

For I myself cannot derive
from the poems I have written
any 'method' which can be applied
to the writing of the next poem;
it comes back, after each poem,
to a level of 'being',
to an almost physical intuition of the time,
or of a form ...
to which I try,
with huge uncertainty,
to be true.
Yours,

Ian[22]

We have a typical case of two complementary ways of
looking at things. We can, first, describe an organism
withconcepts men have developed through contact with
living beings, over the millenia.
In that case we speak of
'living', 'organic function',
'metabolism', 'breathing', 'healing', etc.

Or else we can inquire into causal processes.

Then we use the language of physics and chemistry,
study chemical or electrical processes, for instance,
in nerve conduction,
and assume,
apparently with great success,
that the laws of physics and chemistry,
or more generally the laws of quantum theory,
are fully applicable to living organisms.

These two ways of looking at things are contradictory.
For in the first case,
we can assume that an event is determined
by the purpose it serves, by its goal.

In the second case, we believe that an event is determined
by its immediate predecessor.

It seems most unlikely that both approaches
should have led to the same result by pure chance.

In fact, they compliment each other,
and as we have long since realised,

both are correct precisely because
there is such a thing as life.

Biology thus has no need to ask
which of the two viewpoints is the more correct,
but only how nature managed to arrange things
so that the two should fit together ...

The characteristic biological laws,
for which no analogy can be found in inorganic matter,
result from ...
a complementary situation.[23]

Falke Pisano consistently uses her own voice, as part
of the material needed, in full awareness of its monotone
nature. Besides this, the object requires a listener to
also become part of the material, in order to complete
the construction.

I'd like to use
this space to write a few words about
the background research involved in making our show
at Isabella Bortolozzi gallery in 2006,
and to explain what I call the mechanics of the piece:
how it was supposed to function in that particular context.
Since the piece was about the relation
of the supporting texts that describe artworks
to the artworks themselves—in other words,
how much meaning could be applied to the work
from the outside, the idea of a reference established
by a supporting text, or the text's role in a claim
to legitimate discourse—
we withheld any information outside of
the gallery press release,
which we considered to be an important part of the work.

It was less a technique or theory
than the sensibility of a group of people
that inspired our work.
This sensibility, at once critical and irreverent,
was found in papers associated with a linguistic theory
called generative semantics.
Generative semantics is almost always talked about
in the past tense, sometimes even nostalgically,
because many consider it to be a failed research program,
obsolete or unemployable in present-day linguistic studies.
I would say generative semantics hasn't been
so much discredited as absorbed into a field
that has been completely rearranged or restructured,
partly because of its own impact on that field.

The people who proposed the generative semantics model
saw it as an improvement to
Chomsky's transformational grammar;
they were one-time disciples turned dissidents.
One can safely say that the proponents
of generative semantics were very much aware
of their role as separatists,
or at least of their oppositional position
to the dominant mainstream of Chomsky's theory.
They circulated their ideas in underground papers,
mimeographed them and passed them around.

A SELECTIONAL RESTRICTION INVOLVING PRONOUN CHOICE

YUCK FOO
South Hanoi Institute of Technology

This note is concerned with a counterexample
to the outrageous claim made
by the bourgeois imperialist linguist McCawley
that "there is no verb in English
which allows for its subject just those noun phrases
which may pronominalize to SHE,
namely noun phrases denoting women, ships, and countries ...
selectional restrictions are definable solely
in terms of properties of semantic representation."

Consider the idiomatic sense of "shove X up Y's ass".
(As is well known, Y must be the coreferential
to the indirect object of a deleted performative verb):

(1) Shove it up your/*my ass

(2) He told me to shove it up my/*your ass.

For certain speakers, X may not be a 'full' noun phrase
in surface structure:

(3) Shove your foreign policy up your ass,
you Yankee imperialist.

but all speakers appear to allow X
to be an anaphoric pronoun:

(4) Take your foreign policy and shove it up your ass,
you Yankee imperialist.

The pronoun may be IT but may not be HE or SHE:

(5) Nixon, you imperialist butcher,
take your lunatic Secretary of Defense
and shove him up your ass.

31

(6) Nixon, you imperialist butcher,
take your brainless daughter
and shove her up your ass.

(7) Rockefeller, you robber baron,
take your 80-foot yacht
and shove it/her up your ass.

Certain informants have reported
that they find THEM acceptable
but only when its antecedent is something
whose singular would pronominalize to IT
rather than to HE or SHE:

(8) Nixon, you imperialist butcher,
take your bourgeois lackeys in Taiwan
and shove them up your ass.

(9) Nixon, you oppressor of the masses,
take your anti-crime bills
and shove them up your ass.[24]

The lengthy, spoken nature of the construction's account, and the limits of human memory imply that it can only (must?) take place at the same time as the verbalisation. This sets up a fragile set of circumstances where any flagging of the listener's attention will be responsible for halting the construction of the object.

Ian Hamilton Finlay :

THE CLOUD'S ANCHOR

swallow

Finlay insists, as the Carolingian scholar did,
upon the production of linguistic figures
whose apparent simplicity
is belied by their underlying structure.
In such a work as 'The Cloud's Anchor',
we sense the underlying structure of the figure:

A is to B as C is to D.

(Swallow is to cloud
as anchor is to ship)

The fact that "ship" does not appear in the poem,
and must therefore be inferred [by the reader]
from the reconstruction of the system, is crucial.
Instead of employing metaphor
within an overall discursive flow,
as the traditional poet is bound to do,
Finlay isolates it.

His work consists in
the multiplying of exemplary instances,
through the constant publication of small,
individual works,
rather than the production of more lengthy,
more various and consequently less exemplary ones.

Finlay's enterprise
is a discovery of unity in diversity,
the constant in the changeable.[25]

In sharp contrast to most of the British poets
of his generation, Finlay has pursued a complex
and both aesthetically and ethically difficult course,
navigating between the realms of poetry,
the plastic arts, gardening, and cultural criticism.

Since his turn from strictly verbal to more concrete
modes of poetry, he has created 'poems' in a variety
of media: stone, plaster, bronze, neon, embroidery,
and, most ambitiously, the medium of a full-scale garden,
his Little Sparta, in progress since 1967.

These poems, especially to the extent
that they situate the semantic properties of their words
within a visual and conceptual field,
thereby displacing the purely verbal,
simultaneously return poetry to its etymological roots
as poeisis

—'making'—

and propose a radical redefinition
of the relationship of reader to poem,
a radical renegotiation of the meaning-making contract
implied in the poetic act:
the act of reading a poem is no longer
a matter of making sense
of a given string of verbal signifiers,
but now includes more importantly
the puzzling out of the relationship
among a given set of words
(sometimes, a single word),
the medium in which it is instantiated,
and the surroundings that form its context.[26]

33

As opposed to a process of reading and comprehension,
the temporal nature of listening to the account
makes it impossible to go back and pick up where
one left off, or re-read in order to ensure
understanding.

Many aspects of the art of teaching language skills
have remained a controversy over a period
that encompasses Public education in our democracy.
Among these is the topic of vocalism.
The fact that it has many synonyms, certainly,
has not cleared the education air;
but on the contrary has, perhaps, added to the confusion.
A search of the literature would reveal such synonyms as
implicit speech,
inner speech,
covert language,
inner vocalization,
sub-vocalization,
silent speech,
and vocalism.

The fact that controversy exists,
that some say it is part and parcel
of the reading process, and others say that techniques
should be employed to inhibit its existence,
is ample reason that concerted attempts should be made
to resolve the problem.
Early judgments concerning the role vocalism plays
in the reading process were based on introspection.
Two diametrically opposed views may be represented
by S.S. Stricker and M. Paulhan who gave
their considered opinions during the latter part
of the nineteenth century.
Stricker and his subjects assert that they
could not think of letters or words
without experiencing allied speech-motor phenomena.

On the other hand Paulhan claimed that he COULD
think of anything without experiencing the corresponding
speech-motor phenomena.

Bain, a physiological psychologist,
considered thinking to be
more or less restrained vocalization or acting.

Egger and Ballet,
French psychologists investigating aphasia, announced:
"To read as a matter of fact is
to translate the written word into words to be spoken."

Believing that inner speech may be
a detriment to efficient silent reading,
O'Brien, McDade, and Buswell suggested
a non-oral method of reading instruction.
The results were somewhat inclusive and discouraging.
The non-oral method did not eliminate silent speech
to any greater degree than did other methods.

Anderson and Dearborn and endorsed by Tinker
made a rather revolutionary recommendation:
that vocalism is a desirable, developmental,
learning reinforcement activity,
and that its elimination should not
be prematurely precipitated.

Of interest, at this juncture, is Hollingsworth's
theory of cue-reduction or redintegration
in which a portion of a complex stimulus
would elicit the same response
as the original complex stimulus would evoke.

Early attempts
at measuring vocalism were crude
but rather ingenUous
when consideration is given to the methods
and equipment available.
Curtis placed a tambour on the larynx
and recorded its movements
while the subjects read 'Hiawatha'—

silent reading produced more movements than any other
mental activity.
Only actual whispering produced more.

Parallel to Curtis' work are the results
obtained by Courten by obtaining movements
of the tongue during the performance
of the same activities as Curtis' experimentees.
Courten worked with a rubber bulb on the tongue,
the bulb being connected to a recording tambour.

Probably the first experiments
in which needle electrodes were used
to obtain records of muscular action potentials (MAP)
from the speech musculature were performed by Jacobson
during the early part of the nineteenth century.
The electrodes of fine platinum iridium wires,
were inserted into the muscles of the tongue or lower lip.
The testees in these experiments were instructed
to imagine counting from one upward,
to imagine telling something to a friend,
or think of abstract subjects
such as 'democracy,' 'eternity,' 'electrical resistance,'

and 'Ohm's law,' or the meaning of the words
such as 'incongruous' or 'everlasting.'
The subjects were trained in differential relaxation
or the ability to consciously relax individual muscles
or groups of muscles.

The recordings of the muscles of the tongue or lower lip
of these testees as measured by a galvanometer
indicated very nearly no activity
when the relaxation was called for,
but as soon as a signal was given to perform
the tasks listed previously, electrical activity was noted.

Another study, which certainly is of value to the topic
under discussion, was done by Faaborg-Anderson
on the functioning of the intrinsic laryngeal muscles
in humans.
The aim of this study was to determine the degree
of activity of these muscles as active in the process
of speech, both in the case of healthy persons and
in the case of patients with paresis of the vocal cords.
Silent speech was accompanied by an increase
in electrical activity and action potential
of the laryngeal muscles of both groups.
From the above studies it can be concluded
with confidence that an increase in electric activity
(action potential) in the speech musculature
occurs during certain types of mental activity.
A question may be posed at this point:
"Would there be an increase in muscle action potential (MAP),
which can be called a manifestation
of silent speech or vocalism,
during the process of silent reading ?"[27]

The construction process would be misrepresented
in a book, by simply reprinting the account that is read.
How then, is it possible to engage a reader in a similar
construction on the printed page? How is it possible
to represent the material qualities of Falke Pisano's voice
in the physical space of the book page, as opposed
to the physical space of the exhibition? Is it possible
for YOU the reader to becoME, the/a producer of
material form? In order to retain the position of the reader
in a similar process of the production of material for
another to use.

The twentieth century's obsession
with the impotency
of its own verbal power
has inspired the poet to manipulate
this metaphoric power in new and different ways.

In the present century this linguistic technique
must communicate the figurative meaning
by manipulating the literal object
and it must enrich the poetic structure
by demanding the reader's inference.

Of course metaphor has
traditionally been used in this way.

In addition to such standard usage
however,
metaphor must now function
as vital language once did,

and that is to present the literal images
and to serve as signs
for the concrete 'things'
that words once symbolized.[28]

Would you like to add something?

A lot of things that you were talking about
seem to be hovering around
the 'breakdown' into what
graphic designers' law or discipline involves.
So I think the best way
to address those kinds of issues
is to actually be making projects
like the thing that you're making now,
to put together a magazine
which deals with these issues.

So in some ways,
you're writing a book about writing a book.
And so that's kind of like setting,
that practice,
that putting those ideas into practice
rather than simply describing those ideas.

I think by putting them into practice,
actually making something
that demonstrates the idea
is a very productive way of talking about it.

I think that's the strong part
of what you're going to do
but also I think it underlies
a lot of the things that I do for sure.

I'd rather not talk about it,
I'd rather simply make things,

try to model a certain approach.[29]

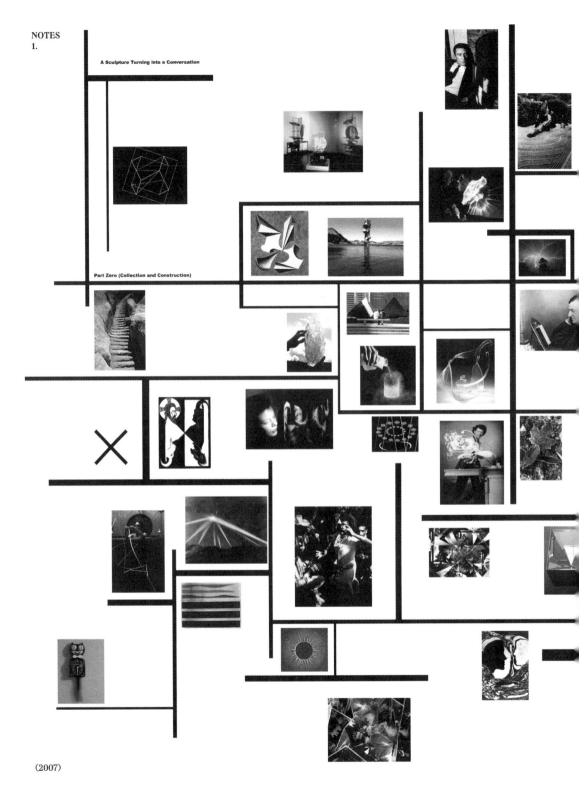

A Sculpture Turning into a Conversation

Part Zero (Collection and Construction)

(2007)

2. Will Holder, in a letter to Stuart Bailey, 14th October, 2008.
3. Will Holder, in a letter to Ian White, 14th July, 2008.
4. Stephen Bann, 'Ian Hamilton Finlay, An Illustrated Essay', Wild Hawthorn Press/ Ceolfrith Press, 1972.
5. Abbie W. Beiman, 'Concrete Poetry: A Study in Metaphor', in Visible Language VIII 3, Summer 1974.
6. Eugen Gomringer, 'Silencio', in Willard Bohn (ed.), 'Modern Visual Poetry', University of Delaware Press, 2001.
7. Beiman.
8. Max Bense, 'Statistical Text', in Solt.
9. Beiman.
10. Noigandres Group, 'Pilot Plan for Concrete Poetry', 1958, in Solt.
11. Mary Ellen Solt (ed.), 'Concrete Poetry, A World View', Indiana University Press, 1968.
12. Haroldo de Campos, 'Alea I—Semantic Variations' (trans. Edwin Morgan), in Solt.
13. Will Holder, in lecture 'Attempt to Evolve X', Somerset House, 29th October 2008.
14. Noigandres Group.
15. Will Holder, 'Attempt to Evolve X'.
16. Noigandres Group.
17. Will Holder, 'Attempt to Evolve X'.
18. Augusto de Campos, 'Brasil/Brazil', in Solt.
19. Oswaldo de Andrade, 'Cannibal Manifesto', www.corpse.org/archives/issue_11/manifestos/ deandrade.
20. Ricardo Basbaum, 'Clark and Oiticica', 2007, www.forumpermanente.org/.painel/coletânea_ho.
21. Hanneke Grootenboer, 'The Rhetoric of Perspective: Realism and Illusionism in Seventeenth-Century Dutch Still-Life Painting', University Of Chicago Press, 2005.
22. Ian Hamilton Finlay, 'Letter to Pierre Garnier, September 17th, 1963', in Solt.
23. Nils Bohr, quoted in Eric Mottram, 'Towards Design in Poetry', Writers Forum, 1977.
24. Jay Chung & Q. Takeki Maeda, 'I'd like to use ...', in Starship magazine, no. 11, 2008.
25. Bann.
26. Mark Scroggins, 'The Piety of Terror: Ian Hamilton Finlay, the Modernist Fragment, and the Neo-classical Sublime' in Flashpoint (online) Spring 1997, Web Issue 1.
27. Donald Cleland, 'Vocalism in Silent Reading', in Visible Language V 2, Spring 1971.
28. Beiman.
29. Alexandre Leray & Stéphanie Vilayphiou, 'Open Source for Graphic Design and Publishing: an interview with David Reinfurt', in Publishing Online, issue #0, from 17–22 March 2008.

LOUD APPLAUSE MARKS THE FINAL BREAK OF THE EVENING, AFTER WHICH THE REMAINING AUDIENCE GATHERS BEFORE MIKE SPERLINGER OF LONDON'S LUX FILM ARCHIVE. HE INTRODUCES THE FOLLOWING FILM FROM THE LEFT LECTERN.

ELEMENTAL PHENOMENON

!! BLOWING IN FOR ONE DAY ONLY !!

"The ease of a child and the spirit of a maelstrom" – "An emotional act of co-ordination and grace"

A GENTLE RAIN. AN AUTUMN BREEZE. A SUDDEN BURST OF SUN.

INTRODUCING

THE TEMPERAMENTAL
BAROMETRIC
CONTOR-
TIONIST!

& HER SYNCHRONISED MERCURIAL CAT

A changeable force commanding atmospheric permutations of unthinkable influence as far as the eye can see. **A PASSING CHILL. A FLASH OF HEAT.** Experience subtle shifts and dramatic modifications. Ups and Downs. Highs and Lows. Come prepared for the most cyclonic show of extremes ever imagined. **THUNDER. LIGHTNING. SEISMIC TREMORS.** INEXHAUSTABLE. INFINITELY VARIED. FEATS TOO NUMEROUS TO RECOUNT.

"Splits body and soul with spiritual excellence ... Torques atmosphere like the muscles in a face."

M S : It's been a long evening and I'm not going to introduce tonight's closing film STEFAN THEMERSON & LANGUAGE at any length, foremost because tonight's other speakers have unwittingly introduced the film already, but also because introducing Stefan Themerson is a daunting task regardless of the time available. He is a polymath, an utterly multi-faceted Renaissance Man, a key figure in almost any interesting history of 20th century European art, and still remarkably relatively unknown. A final, more personal reason is that Jasia Reichardt—who runs the Themerson archive in London—is sitting in front of me, and she has forgotten more about the Themersons than I will ever know.

However, for those of you that aren't familiar with the Themersons at all, Stefan and his partner Franciszka grew up in Poland, where they made a series of important avant-garde films in the 1930s. They were part of a community of ground-breaking experimental filmmakers and artists in Poland at the time. During the Second World War they relocated to London, where their activities were more focused around writing and publishing, mainly through their own imprint, Gaberbocchus Press.

The film is directed by Erik van Zuylen, a Dutch filmmaker. It's a quasi-collaborative 40-minute documentary in which Stefan Themerson and an interlocuter discuss Semantic Poetry, one of Themerson's inventions which has cropped up in previous issues of DOT DOT DOT. I want to propose 3 reasons for showing this film right now. The first is related to a publishing project I'm working on at Lux, based on artists' writing about the moving image. Themerson's writing will hopefully infiltrate this project, and here I'll just point you in the direction of an important text he wrote about making films, called THE URGE TO CREATE VISIONS.

The second, again more parochial reason for showing the film here is because there's a direct relationship between Themerson's work and DOT DOT DOT's agenda. The film begins, for instance, with a definition of the word 'definition', and many of the later entanglements of semantic translation work with a spiralling self-consciousness familiar to DOT DOT DOT —a discourse which is always to a higher power.

The last reason that I think this film is particularly pertinent right now is because of the questions it poses about poetry and power. A few of you here may have recently seen a show here in London by Emily Wardill at Jonathan Viner's gallery, which contained a 16mm film called 'Sea Oak'—an imageless film with a forty minute soundtrack. This is a recording of an interview with group of theorists and social scientists in California who were part of the now-defunct Rockridge Institute. They are talking about the fact that, in American politics at least, right wing politicians had a very instinctive understanding that power was connected not just to rhetoric but also to symbolism and affect—and to a particular use of language founded even on intonation. The implication, then, is that by comparison Democratic politicians were tone deaf: they didn't understand this other power of language that had nothing to do with rational argument.

With this in mind, the discourse in STEFAN THEMERSON & LANGUAGE is deceptively simple and extraordinarily relevant. Something particularly notable happens in the middle of the film. It's a moment when, on a park bench, the interlocutor begins to question the model of Semantic Poetry which Themerson appears to have set up in opposition to political oratory, or the oratory of power, and suggests that there's a certain complicity between that power and poetry. Ultimately the film suggests how we might begin to unfold that complicity, and examine how poetry might deal with its entanglement with power.

It's important to understand that Themerson's argument is animated by a very powerful irony—one which I'm going to dare to suggest is a Romantic irony, and even a German Romantic irony, in the most 19th century sense. When he talks about revealing the unseen truth of a proposition, Themerson isn't talking about a psychoanalytic model. Rather, you begin to realise that his talking about clarification of meaning is essentially parodic: the clarification that is actually happening is rather that it's impossible to clarify meaning; that meaning is always going to escape and proliferate.

Finally, there are subtitles, so if you're sitting behind someone very tall or wearing a hat you might wish to relocate. I hope you enjoy the film.

THE FILM PLAYS. THE CAST ARE VISIBLY READING FROM THE FOLLOWING SCRIPT, SUPPLIED HERE BY ERIK VAN ZUYLEN. THIS VERSION OMITS AN INTERVIEW SEQUENCE WITH A PUBLIC ORATOR BUT INCLUDES A RE-SCRIPTED FINAL PAGE (14) FOLLOWED BY THE FILM'S CLOSING FRAMES: A MULTIPLE TRANSLATION OF THE DUTCH NATIONAL ANTHEM.

<u>STEFAN THEMERSON & language</u>   script for TV
                                       by Erik van Zuylen

Dramatis Personae:

The Poet   ...   Mr. Stefan Themerson
The Interviewer   ...   Mr. Gerard Stigter
The Singer   ...
The Orator   ...   Mr. Stoelmann Leysner
The Pianoplayer

1) A parc. S.T. & G.S. walking towards the round pavilion
   intended for musxax musical performances in the open air.
   S.T.: Shall we take a seat in the rear?

   The singer & the pianoplayer come down from the podium,
   smiling, shake hands with S.T., ignore G.S.

   They lead S.T. to a chair in the middle of the podium.

   The singer starts adressing the audience:

Singer: Ladies and gentlemen! It is my pleasure to sax welcome
(dutch) the poet who will read from his work in a few moments!

      He He nods to his left where S.T. is sitting.

   S.T. looks over his shoulder at the person on his left, the
   pianoplayer, 'not without curiosity'. The player smiles back.

SINGER: I don't have to tell you what a poet is, but I will
(dutch) sing it for you, in the words of the poet himself, or
         rather in the words of his dictionary, because the text
         of this song is the complete and precise definition of
         the words: I am a young poet.

   Insert: the book on the piano, rexvealing title & author.
           while the pianoplayer starts the preludium.

SINGER: (sings) I am a young human being (3x)
                 Who practises literary composition,
                 Forming a unity in itself,
                 Written in a metrical form,
                 Rhymed or unrhymed, Good or Bad,
                 Mark'd by high powers of imagination
                 And great beauty of language;

SINGER: Words and music by Stefan Themerson!
    The singer makes a littke bow to his ~~right~~ left. Applause.

    S.T. has a puzzled look on his face. He looks over his left
    shoulder. The pianoplayer smiles back and claps his hands.

SINGER: Words have a certain meaning which can be expressed
(dutch) by their definition. I shall now read to you the
        definition of 'definition'.   (He opens the dictionary)

Insert: definition in the dictionary.

SINGER: Definition: an ~~exact~~ explanation of the exact meaning
(dutch) of a word, term, or frase. (He closes the dictionary)
        It is possible to express yourself by means of a
        composition of words, 'the language', in a clear and
        unambiguous way, but not everybody is doing so. Some
        people are merely incapable, others are unwilling to
        do so, and for different reasons.
        In the first place there are the poets who use rhyme
        and a compelling cadance in their verses. In his book
        'On Semantic Poetry' Stefan Themerson says:
    The singer makes a little bow on his left while mentioning
    S.T.'s name.

    S.T.: What the devil can Semantic Poetry be?(He looks at the
~~SINGER~~ pianoplayer for an answer. The player nods & smiles back)
SINGER: Stefan Themerson ~~says~~ says: (he reads)
(dutch) By concepts produced by poets I don't mean their rhymes.
        We are not interested in rhymes. On the contrary.
        Rhymes are what we are not interested in. They are the
        opium of the people. An outmoded L.S.D.
        A good pair of rhymes induces us to accept any silly
        statement as something beautiful and true, and - before
        we have time to realize that we have been taken in -
        the rhythm of the lines has already carried us on to
        the next pair'
            (he closes the book)

SINGER: Secondly there are the orators, the demagogues
(dutch) who make use of similar techniques. (he opens the
dictionary)

Insert: 'demagogue' in the dictionary.

SINGER: Demagogy is : The art of leading the people -mostly
(dutch) used in a bad sense- factious oratorship; playing on
the passions, prejudices and ignorance of the masses
to win their support.
As a remedy against this sort of poetry and those
orators, Stefan Themerson (makes a little bow to the
left) has developed a form of poetry which he called
Semantic Poetry.

S.T. shakes his head in disapproval. He looks over left shoulder.
The pianoplayer smiles and nods back.

S.T.: No, I'm afraid there is no remedy for that sort of thing.
It is not a remedy but a 'method' of revealing (perhaps
with a poker-face kind of humor) the unseen truth
about a proposition. In one case it may be debunking a
statement, in another case it may be -on the contrary- enhancing, enriching it.

SINGER: As a 'method' of revealing the unseen truth about a
(dutch) proposition, Stefan Themerson has developed a form
of poetry which he called Semantic Poetry.

S.T.: Each of the words (in Semantic Poetry) should have
one and only one meaning. They should be well defined.
They should be washed clean of all those diverse
aureolas which depend on the condition of the market.
The word 'war', for instance, carries with it
different associations for different people. Thus, it is
good for a political speech, but in a poem I would
prefer to find instead a more exxact definition, for
instance, that in my dictionary: The open conflict
between nations, or active international hostility
carried on by force of arms.

Insert: 'war' in the dictionary.

                                        Fade out.

Fade in.

Title: THE WORD 'WAR' USED IN POLITICAL & RELIGIOUS SPEECHES.

(dutch) Sequence of material from old news reals, showing
orators at work: Charles de Gaulle, Billy Graham,
Spiro Agnew. They all use the word 'war'.

Insert: text in the book Bayamus.

S.T.: (reads) ... in a poem I would prefer to find instead
a more exact definition, for instance, that in my
Dictionary...

G.S. approaches S.T. from behind. He startles S.T. by his
adress.

G.S.: Mr. Themerson! In your books you prove to have a
sharp, analytical mind...

S.T.: (strongly denying) I don't know about that!

G.S. opens a folding-chair and sits down, the back of the
chair in front of him.

S.T.: And the very fact that I am not capable of analysing
my mind (or rather that my mind cannot analyse itself)
indicates that it is not analytical.
(thus proving himself innocent, he smiles)

G.S.: (leaning forward, the clever interrogator) But does
analytical mean 'capable to analyse itself'? What if
I said: 'you have a sharp knife' and you would answer
by: 'it is not sharp at all, it can't even cut itself!!'

S.T.: I don't even know whether it is my mind or the rest of my
body that feels irritated when noticing a discrepancy
between what is said about a situation and the reality
of the situation, - the itch that causes a restless
desire to reveal the truth by scratching the form and
revealing the content. (S.T. has cleverly indicated

Qzâzx that there is an analogy between his own and the
interrogator's purpose) (G.S. nods approvingly)

G.S.: As a starting point for those analyses you have often
introduced a situation in which a police officer is
examining a suspect. (This does nod plead for S,T.)

(S.T. frankly admits this fact, it proves his point)

S.T.: Now, if I have used police interrogations in a number
of my writings, it was precisely because that sort of
dialogue shows where even the most matter-of-fact
logic of language does not fit the truth of the
situation.

G.S.: (innocent catch question) How would you describe the
situation in which we are now?

S.T.: It reminds me of a situation which I described 30
years ago in my book Bayamus. (he opens the book)
'After some adventures with the three-legged Bayamus
who perambulates about past-war London on a rollerskate
attached to his middle leg, I found myself in the
Theatre of Semantic Poetry.
I intended to enter the Theatre quietly, without
attracting anybody's attention, and to sit somewhere
at the end of the auditorium. But when we found ourselves
in the wide open door, I saw the eyes of some hunderd
people directed towards us.
At the same moment two men in evening dress approached
us with gestures of welcome.
They showed me the chair in the middle, and when I sat
down I saw that instead of being in the audience I was
facing it from the platform.
I looked at the gentleman on my left and at the
gentleman on my right and was unsure. I was wondering
which of them was the poet when a terrible suspicion
came over my mind.
'Well,' I said to myself, 'and what if I promised to
hold this recital and forgot all about it?'
(he pauses, looking at G.S., turning a page.)

SINGER: I am convinced that the poetry which is going to be delivered
(dutch) here in a moment, will open a new era in the understanding of language. And I'm also convinced that by
understanding our language better, we will better
understand ourselves, and our world.

S.T.: (reading) The gentleman on my right was finishing his
      speech. He said one more sentence, there was something
      in it about a new world, and he sat down. The whole
      audience was waiting now and I had no doubt it was my
      turn.
   (the singer acts as described. S.T. rises)
      I rose. In spite of everything it was rather funny to
      see all these people waiting for your poems, while you
      had no poems to recite.
   (he looks at G.S., smiles, unsure if it is as funny as
   described, looks at the pianoplayer, thesinger, the waiting
   audience, walks towards the desk, facing the audience.)
S.T.: My Lord Archbishop, Your Excellencies, Your Graces, (pause)
      My Lords, Ladies and Gentlemen, Men and Women, Children...
      (pause) Embryos, if any; Spermatozoa reclining at the
      edge of your chairs; all living Cells; Bacteria; Viruses;
      Molecules of Air, and Dust, and Water, -I feel much
      honoured in being asked to address you all and to recite
      poetry,- but I have no poetry to recite.
   (reading for himself from the book)
      'I have no poetry to recite,' I repeated. And suddenly
      I felt that it was not true. My memory started to work,
      and I knew that something was being formed in it. Now
      it was necessary to gain time.
   (adressing the people)
      I have no poems to recite, but I may give you the
      instrumentation, the orchestration of...
   (for himself)
      In that moment everything became clear to me.
   (he turns to the blackboard, shows the side on which the
   first bars of the polish song are written, the melody
   and the chords for piano under it. The pianoplayer
   illustrates what S.T. indicates.)
      Well, you may read a musical score horizontally,
      following the melodic line, and you may read it
      vertically, following the chord structure.

S.T.: The same with poetry. You may read horizontally the
melody of a poem, but you may also take each of its
words and score it vertically for your whole intellectual
orchekxstra, you may give each of them the flesh of
of exact definition; instead of allowing them to
evoke the clichés stored in your mind, you may try to
find the true reality to which every word points, and that
is what I call Seamntic Poetry.
Semantic Poetry's business is to translate poems
not from one tongue into another but from a language
composed of words so poetic that they have lost their
impact, - into something that will give them a new meaning
and flavor.
Avant-garde got to go back to Diderot, yes, Denis, of
all people, to the time when men and women tried to
think, yes, think, and it should start from there again.

SINGER: (interrupting) Well, your damn' thinking didn't
prevent the war, did it?

S.T.: (shouting back) Well, did your damn' singing?

(The pianoplayer strikes the first chords of 'How nice
it is'. The singer starts singing,)

SINGER: Jak to na wojence źadnie   (2x)
         Kiedy uźan z konia spadnie   (2x)
         Koledzy go nie żałują   (2x)
         Jeszcze końmi potratują   (2x)

S.T.: This is a polish popular song, the words of which put
into English as literally as possible, are:
How nice it is when during a little war

SINGER: (sings translation)
Wat leuk als in een oorlogje

S.T.: The Uhlan falls from his horse

SINGER: Een Ulaan van z'n paard af valt

S.T.: His comrades don't regret him

SINGER: Zijn kameraden treuren niet

S.T.: They even trample him

SINGER: Zij lopen hem onder de voet

S.T.:   Ladies and gentlemen, that melody gives a very high
patriotkic emotion to anyone who listens to it or
sings it; it gives a joyful feeling, briskness,
sprightliness, and I would like to call it a
physiological song, unless scored for the more
intellectual orchestra of the Semantic Poetry
translation.

(each line is preceded by the corresponding bars,
played on the piano)

(each line is illustrated :

The first lines by showing the corresponding text
& typography in the book.

The other lines by showing illustrations from an
encyclopaedia-Diderot?-)

S.T. is sitting on a bench in the parc, smoking his pipe.
G.S. approaches him.

    G.S.: You've done some fine oratory yourself, Mr. Themerson.

    S.T.: Thank you.

    G.S.: Do you mind if I sit down.

    S.T.: Not at all.

    G.S.: I've written down some questions.

    S.T.: I've written down some answers.

    G.S.: Let's see if they fit in with each other.

    S.T.: All right.

    G.S.: You have accused the orators that they have stolen the devices of your tools, the tools of a poet. But Now, was it ever your intention to use those tools?

    S.T.: It was never my intention, but they were just my tools!

    G.S.: I have discovered something. In this book, Word PLay by Peter Farb, the author mentions the way in which American officials tried to minimize the Viet-nam War, it says:"
"not a <u>war</u> according to the Pentagon but an <u>international armed conflict</u>"
So what they did was using the definition as an euphemism!(A mild expression for one that is offensive.)
And we see a kind of reversal of your method of 'debunking a statement by translating it into its definition'. Those Senators who wanted to debunk the statement 'it is merely an international armed conflict' said in a dramatic & threatening way: 'there is a war going on!'

Title: THE WORD <u>WAR</u> USED TO DEBUNK THE STATEMENT:
    'IT IS MERELY AN INTERNATIONAL ARMED CONFLICT'
Fragment of a speech of Edward Kennedy on the war.

G.S.: What's your reaction on this process of reversion?

S.T.: That's perhaps one of the things that made me say
that Semantic Poetry Translation is not a Remedy
but a Method. It can be used one way or another.
And ítxkz whichever way it is used - it is
profitable to translate it into its opposite.
Because it is profitable to show more than one
aspect of things. "Because the world is more
complicated than our truth about it." If I may
quote myself...

G.S.: 'Wooff wooff or who killed Richard Wagner' page 42...

S.T.: Indeed...

G.S.: About those leaders. If they want the people to
be emotionally involved they use the word 'war'.
If they want to keep a war distant and the people
uninterested by not evoking kxx any emotions or
associations they use the definition 'international
armed conflict'. It seems that after having stolen
the devices of the 'classical' poets, the orators
now are stealing the devices of the 'semantic' poet.

S.T.: Some naïve semanticists believe that if only our
leaders (of all sorts) could understand the meaning
of their own pronouncements, they would amend their
ways. What an illusion! The leaders know the
mechanism of language much better than all semanticists,
linguistic philosophers, and logical formalists
put together. It's only that they use their knowledge
for their own purpose.

G.S.: Which means that they are fully responsable for their
actions. Well, Mr. Themerson, thank you for your
cooperation, you have been quite helpful.

(he rises) I can assure you that I'll probe this matter to the
very bottom. I'm going to have a little chat with the
people you accuse. See you later.

(he walks away, then suddenly stops, slaps his forehead, turns)

ꞔzꞮzꞮ
G.S.: One last question: Do you think there exists a mutual
understanding between the demagxogues and their
victims? Let's say a kind of consensus?
Complicity perhaps?
S.T.: (slightly nodding) Hélas!
G.S.: (nods, walks away)

G.S. & S.T. are walking along the beach. The wind disturbs the sheets of
paper from which they are reading their lines.

G.S.:   I have investigated your allegations concerning the orators,
the demagogues and the religious leaders.
Suppose I've found some proof, I'm still wondering...
What if the orators add beauty to their language by using
alliterations, what if they make themselves clear by using
metaphores? Why would it be permitted to a poet and not to
an orator?

S.T.:   This beauty of langauge! Ha! That's exactly what irritates my
nervous system, because it is used to conceal the truth of the
the situation! Would you be so kind to give me the definition of
demagogy?

G.S.:   Playing on the passions, prejudices and ignorance of the people
masses to win their support.

S.T.:   Exactly. And now you have seen something of the mechanism behind
it. The orator adds beauty to his speech and by doing so he
plays on the passions of the people. When they are moved by
a pronouncement, they will accept it as true.
The orator tajlks about beliefs and by confirming the people in
their prejudices, he will get those beliefs accepted as facts.
The orator uses his knowledge to keep the people in ignorance.
And it is useless to talk about 'should it be permitted'.
It shouldn't off course. But there is no way to stop it.
You can only try to expose it whenever it occurs.

G.S.:   Yes.
Please look at those dunes, Mr. Themerson. They are hills, lying
in rows along the sea, hills which originated from loose sand,
blown together by the wind.
But in the minds of many people they are a national symbol.
There is a popular song about the White Top Of The Dunes and
we have applied on it your method of Semantic Poetry Translation.

ST: That's a good question./ Indeed:/ Why should what is good for a Poet/not be good for an Orator ?// Do you remember how you defined Demagogy ?

GS: "Playing on the passions, prejudices and ignorance of the masses to win their support".

ST: Well, there you are.// When a poet,/ or a novelist,/ becomes a demagogue,/ the same applies to him.// Poetry as well as Politics may be morally vicious / and intellectually dishonest.|| In such cases,/ both Poetry and Oratory - political, religious, philosophical, - are like Crime.|| The greater a crime is,/ the more impressive it is, but the less excusable.

GS: Are you a moralist ?

ST: Did you say: 'humourist' ?

GS: No, I said: 'moralist'.

ST: Oh no, I'm not a moralist./ I'm too old to be a moralist. But it irritates my Skin when the Beauty of Language is used to conceal the Truth of a Situation. And that's precisely what a Demagogue does.

A demagogue, (whether he is a politician or a poet,/ a prophet or a novelist) - adds beauty to his speech,/ and/by doing so/plays on people's passions. // When they are moved by what he says,/they accept it as true./ He talks about Beliefs,/and by confirming people in there Prejudices,/gets those beliefs accepted/as facts./ He uses his skill to hide from people either his bad logic,/or his tendencious premisses,/ - or both. //

And it is useless to talk about 'Should it be permitted?' You and I, we can only say that we don't like it. But there is no/way/to stop it.|| We can only expose it when it occurs.//

GS: Yes.
Please....&c....

Waar het witachtig blinkende
hoogste punt
van de
in rijen
langs de zee
liggende
heuvels

where the whitish summit

aan de voet van
de
in
rijen
langs
de
zee
liggende
heuvels

while standing at the foot of
the row of hills along the coast

Waar het witachtig blinkende
hoogste punt
van de
in rijen
langs de zee
liggende
heuvels

of the row of hills along the coast

comprising fine sand
assembled by the wind

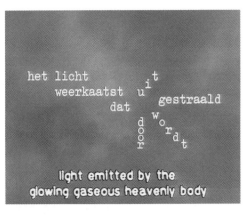

het licht
weerkaatst uit gestraald
dat wordt door

light emitted by the
glowing gaseous heavenly body

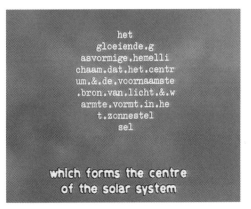

het
gloeiende.g
asvormige.hemelli
chaam.dat.het.centr
um.&.de.voornaamste
.bron.van.licht.&.w
armte.vormt.in.he
t.zonnestel
sel

which forms the centre
of the solar system

around which the earth revolves

zodat
de ogen
van de
toeschouwer
pijnlijk
worden
geprikkeld

reflects painfully into
the eyes of the viewer

En de 575000 km^2
grote zoute watervlakte
randzee
van
de Atlantische Oceaan
omgrensd door

and the 575000 km2
salt water surface

Scandinavië
de   Jutland
Britse   Duitsland
eilanden   Nederland
België

branch of the Atlantic Ocean
bordered by Scandinavia

Scandinavië
de   Jutland
Britse   Duitsland
eilanden   Nederland
België

Jutland, Germany, Holland,
Belgium and Britain

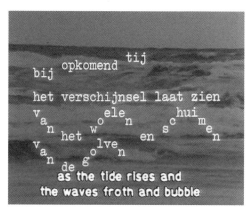

bij opkomend tij
het verschijnsel laat zien
van ele hui
het wo en m
va lve en
n de g
n

as the tide rises and
the waves froth and bubble

---

door
breking
of door
botsing
van de
aanrollende
en
teruggekaatste
as they break or clash
with each other

---

op
de
nauwe
grens tussen de zee
en het
aangewaaide
het door
inpoldering
verworven
land
on the narrow boundary between
the sea and the silt

---

op
de
nauwe
grens tussen de zee
en het
aangewaaide
het door
inpoldering
verworven
land
the land acquired
by polder-forming

---

waarbij de
toehoorder
de indruk krijgt
dat het geraas
van de branding
een betuiging inhoudt van

the viewer gains the impression
that the breakers

waarbij de
toehoorder
de indruk krijgt
dat het geraas
van de branding
een betuiging inhoudt van

express polite good-nature
or respect

beleefdheid
vriendschap
of eerbied
zoals bij personen die elkaar
ontmoeten of
uit elkaar gaan

like people greeting or
saying farewell

Geef ik in LUIDE KLANKEN
mijn vreugde
te kennen
terwijl ik
mij bevind
op dat deel
van de
zeebodem
zonder verheffing of diepten

I express my joy LOUDLY

Geef ik in LUIDE KLANKEN
mijn vreugde
te kennen
terwijl ik
mij bevind
op dat deel
van de
zeebodem
zonder verheffing of diepten
while standing on that part of
the sea bed without dips or rises

dat alleen bij hoog water
door de zee
overspoeld
wordt

and which is only covered
by the sea at high tide

Geef ik
in vrolijk geroepen woorden

RUCHTBAARHEID

aan mijn gevoel
van blijdschap
terwijl ik
mij bevind

In cheerful words I DIVULGE
my happiness

Geef ik
in vrolijk geroepen woorden

RUCHTBAARHEID

aan mijn gevoel
van blijdschap
terwijl ik
mij bevind

while standing at the foot of
the row of hills along the coast

taan
ont s or d e
o n d o
j n e t v a n f i j w i
die zi h n wind
door e v n z a
samenstui a n d

comprising fine sand
assembled by the wind

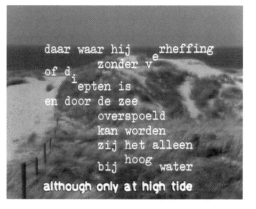

daar waar hij   rheffing
          zonder v^e
of d_i
    epten is
en door de zee
        overspoeld
        kan worden
        zij het alleen
           hoog

**where it has no dips or rises
and can be flooded by the sea**

---

daar waar hij   rheffing
          zonder v^e
of d_i
    epten is
en door de zee
        overspoeld
        kan worden
        zij het alleen
      bij hoog water

although only at high tide

oes   voo
k t   r
i een warme u

**I cherish a warm affection
for you**

---

oh Koninkrijk der Nederlanden
    constitutionele
    erfelijke monarchie
    in West-Europa

oh Kingdom of the Netherlands

oh Koninkrijk der Nederlanden
    constitutionele
    erfelijke monarchie
    in West-Europa

**constitutional hereditary monarchy
in Western Europe**

---

grenzend aan
de Noordzee   Duitsland
            België
beroemd door
      haar boter en kaas
      haar klompen
      haar bollenvelden
      haar gedistilleerd

**bordering Germany,
the North Sea and Belgium**

---

grenzend aan
de Noordzee   Duitsland
            België
beroemd door
      haar boter en kaas
      haar klompen
      haar bollenvelden
      haar gedistilleerd

**famous for its butter and
cheese and clogs**

---

grenzend aan
de Noordzee   Duitsland
            België
beroemd door
      haar boter en kaas
      haar klompen
      haar bollenvelden
      haar gedistilleerd

its tulip fields and liquor

ik voel
e e n o n v b a nd m e t
k e l i j k e r
b re-

I feel an unbreakable
bond with you

oh land dat met recht laag
genoemd wordt
omdat
bij afwezigheid van
de dijken
de zeeweringen

oh country so rightly
known as low

oh land dat met recht laag
genoemd wordt
omdat
bij afwezigheid van
de dijken
de zeeweringen

because without the dikes
and sea walls

de
in
rijen
langs
de
zee
liggende
heuvels

and the row of hills
along the coast

de helft van
uw landoppervlakte
overspoeld
zou worden
en u opnieuw
prijsgegeven zou zijn aan
een natuurlijk
proces van

half of your surface area
would be flooded

de helft van
uw landoppervlakte
overspoeld
zou worden
en u opnieuw
prijsgegeven zou zijn aan
een natuurlijk
proces van

and you would again be subjected
to a natural process

het aanslibben van modder
het aanspoelen van stenen
meegevoerd door de grote
rivieren
het aanwaaien van zand
en de vervening van
o n a f z i e n b a r e
moerassen

silting up of mud and stones
from the rivers

het aanslibben van modder
het aanspoelen van stenen
meegevoerd door de grote
rivieren
het aanwaaien van zand
en de vervening van
o n a f z i e n b a r e
moerassen

the blown sand and fen
forming in vast marshes

ON THIS DAY ONLY, Welcome with *Disbelief—*

LIKE THE TRUEST OF SCALES

AND FAIREST OF BEAUTIES,

THIS POLYGRAPHIC WONDER

PERFORMS THE MOST DELICATE BALANCING ACT,

SWOONING

IN THE FACE OF **ANY** UNTRUTH!

WHITE LIES, BLACK LIES, COMPLEX AND ELABORATE LIES — LIES TOLD TO PROTECT, LIES TOLD TO ENCHANT,

LIES TOLD IN PURSUIT — EVASIONS, EXAGGERATIONS, EQUIVOCATIONS — FALSE MODESTIES, INSINCERITIES, SELF-AGGRANDISEMENTS

— HARMLESS LIES AND HURTFUL LIES — LIES TOLD BY OMISSION, LIES TOLD TO ONESELF —

INDEED, ALL FORMS OF FALSEHOOD!

Compensating With EQUAL & OPPOSITE Measure For EACH & EVERY Deception

HER HEARTBEAT SLOWS, HER BREATH SHALLOWS;
HER VISION DIMS, HER PALLOR ASHENS

AND HER DIVINE, SOOTHSAYING BODY

crumples to the ground.

A HEROINE

OF THE SINCEREST BENEVOLENCE AND MOST INFALLIBLE COMPASSION

WITNESS THIS INCREDULOUS SPECTACLE OF STAGGERING

! ! EQUILIBRIUM ! !

FAINTGIRL

THE SAME LOCATION, THURSDAY 30 OCTOBER. 7PM.

INT. REORIENTED TO THE SOUTH TOWARDS A BACKDROP OF TRANSLUCENT WHITE
CURTAINS HEAVILY LIT BY TWIN SPOTLIGHTS FROM THE BACK OF THE ROOM.

TONIGHT'S AUDIENCE CONGREGATES TO THE FAINT SOUND OF MARCEL DUCHAMP'S
'LA MARIÉE MISE A NU PAR SES CELIBATAIRES, MEME' ['THE BRIDE STRIPPED BARE
BY HER BACHELORS, EVEN'] AS PERFORMED AND RECORDED BY MATS PERSSON AND
KRISTINE SCHOLZ.

etc.

D AND S APPROACH THE LECTERNS FROM THE BAR AS THE MUSIC FADES OUT TO
SILENCE. THEY PROCEED TO DELIVER, WORD FOR WORD, THE SAME INTRODUCTION
AS YESTERDAY EVENING. D CONTINUES, RE-AMPLIFIED IN STEREO.

D : Tonight's first piece comprises a set of spoken liner notes to the LP 'From Brussels with Love', originally released in 1983 on cassette tape and reissued last year on CD. Dan Fox originally recorded a demo version of these notes, titled REFRACTED LIGHT THROUGH ARMOURY SHOW, earlier this year at the 7th Regiment Armory Building in New York, which was then released as a hard-panned stereo MP3. Here he reads an extended version of the original. Dan

D IS INTERRUPTED FROM BEHIND THE RIGHT-HAND LECTERN BY A BLAST OF WHAT
SOUNDS LIKE WHITE NOISE OR RADIO STATIC.

UNSEEN, DAN FOX BEGINS READING INTO A MIC. FROM THE BACK OF THE ROOM,
HIS VOICE AMPLIFIED THROUGH THE LEFT SPEAKER, WITH VARIOUS EXCERPTS OF
MUSIC AND OTHER SPOKEN WORD RECORDINGS THROUGH THE RIGHT ONE.

L : I move the radio dial from left to right.
First slowly, teasing out liquid from prickly
static. Then sending it spinning back, right
to left, thudding and juddering across
frequency bumps until it hits distant pulses
and dispassionate voices intoning numerical
instructions, perhaps to sleeper agents for
whom email and digital radio are still the stuff
of a dashed-off 1950s sci-fi story …

R :

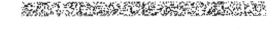

A New York station is calling. I pick up the
analysis of a transmission that has been
circulating since 1913.

According to 'New Yorker' columnist and art
critic Calvin Tomkins, "Only one-third of the
1,300 works of art on view came from Europe,
but they outsold the local product by more
than two to one—of the 174 works sold, 123
were by foreign artists. Seen in the context of
advanced Modernism, American art suddenly
looked backward and banal, at least to the
small group of collectors for whom the Armory

Show came as a great beam of light in the future. John Quinn, the brilliant New York lawyer who had helped to organize the show was the largest single buyer—he spent a total of $5,808.75 for works by Derain, Pascin, Redon, Segonzac, Villon, Duchamp-Villon, and other European and American artists. The second biggest buyer, a Chicago lawyer named Arthur Jerome Eddy, traveled to New York for the show and acquired, among other things, two of the four paintings submitted by Marcel Duchamp: 'Portrait of Chess Players' and 'The King & Queen Surrounded by Swift Nudes'. The Duchamp brothers all did remarkably well. Raymond sold three of the four sculptures he had sent over, Jacques Villon sold all nine of his paintings, and Marcel ended up selling four out of four. The infamous 'Nude Descending a Staircase' found its buyer near the end of the show's New York run, when a San Francisco antiques dealer named Frederic C. Torrey, en route home from his visit to the Armory Show, suddenly had a brainstorm. He got off the train in Albuquerque, New Mexico, and sent a telegram to Walter Pach saying, 'I will buy Duchamp Nude Woman Descending Stairway please reserve.'"

Well, was it Oscar Wilde or Clement Greenberg who said "To be popular one must be a mediocrity"? OH ARMOURY SHOW. The 1913 International Exhibition of Modern Art, held at the 69th Regiment Armory, New York, "wasn't well accounted for in Paris", recalled Duchamp. "I don't think there was even a newspaper account of it, except for short notes." Surprising given that, when the exhibition hit Chicago, art students hanged effigies of Constantin Brancusi and Henri Matisse in protest.

But no surprise, Marcel, when you consider that America can't even agree on what you look like:
"Quite handsome, with blond, curly hair … Could be taken for a well-groomed Englishman rather than a Frenchman" says the 'Tribune'. 'Arts & Decoration' has you down with "red hair, blue eyes, freckles, a face … and a figure that would seem American even among Americans." And the U.S. Immigration and Naturalization Service holds that you're 5 feet 10 inches, fair, with brown hair and 'chestnut' eyes.

The Armory Show is widely regarded as American art's seismic schism with its past, the moment at which the shock troops of the European avant-garde arrived to drag U.S.

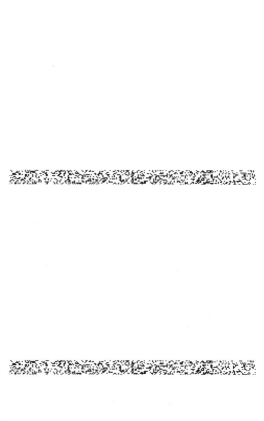

artists kicking and screaming into the 20th century. But you Marcel, living in New York, in exile from Old Europe, you exhort us to "Look at the skyscrapers!" "Has Europe anything to show more beautiful than these?" you ask. "New York itself is a work of art, a complete work of art ... And I believe that the idea of demolishing old buildings, old souvenirs, is fine ... The dead should not be permitted to be so much stronger than the living. We must learn to forget the past, to live in our own time." Europe watches America. Does Europe realize that America is returning this stare? This is the start of a special relationship.

I nudge the radio dial a few kilohertz higher, to broadcasting stations east of New York, north of 1913. The blades of a steely synthesizer melody slide through the static.

John Foxx, A JINGLE #1 ⸺

THE LIGHTS GO OUT. A DETAIL OF A ROUNDEL FROM A STAINED GLASS WINDOW AT THE 7TH REGIMENT ARMORY BUILDING IS SLIDE-PROJECTED AT AN OBLIQUE ANGLE ONTO THE WHITE CURTAINS. SOMEWHERE NEAR THE FRONT A FOG MACHINE EMITS A LARGE CLOUD OF DRY ICE WHICH CURLS UP THROUGH THE HARSH LIGHT TOWARDS THE CEILING. THIS CONTINUES INTERMITTENTLY THROUGHOUT.

Do we ever read the airwaves? Or do we stamp them out at street level? I turn the radio dial ... but who am I kidding? This is 2008. You can tune straight in. There's no fuzz or crackle. There are no spitting frequencies. There are just immaculate surfaces of digital broadcast and 24/7 accessibility. In a one-zero-one age of access to every age, once-chill signifiers of technocratic progress, once-gleaming beacons of Modernism have evanesced into a new kind of language static to makes the hairs stand up on the back of your neck. Control has enabled the abandoned wires again at street level. Comb your hair and stick on a grey raincoat. The vocab's simple: RADIO, CABLE, TELEX, MOSCOW, BERLIN, VIENNA, PARIS, AGENT, STATION, OBSERVATORY, STEEL, UTOPIA, FUTURE, PLASTIC, BAUHAUS, GEOMETRIC, ANGULAR, ABSTRACTION, FUNCTIONALITY, RADIOACTIVITY, ENERGY, ANTENNA, RECEIVER, TRANSISTOR, TRANSMISSION, BROADCAST, HOVER-PORT, MONO-RAIL, FACTION, DIVISION, BLOC, UNDERGROUND, SECRET, EXPRESSWAY, FREEWAY, HIGHWAY, AUTOBAHN, TRANS-EUROPE, TRANS-ATLANTIC, TRANS-, PLANS-, AUTO-, MOBILE-, DUCHAMP ...

... Hang on, is that your face I see Marcel? Or is it Vladimir Tatlin? I thought you were supposed to be in America? At least, I think it's **63**

your face, Marcel—I have it in my hands.
It's staring out from a deluxe booklet
accompanying the album 'From Brussels with
Love', a compilation of distinctly somber,
melancholy, Northern European post-punk
songs, poetry and interviews. It was released
on cassette tape in 1980 by the Belgian
record label Les Disques du Crépuscule,
sister label to Manchester's Factory Records.
Your portrait, Marcel, is slavishly copied
from a photograph in black-and-white ink by
a hand trained in the school of school exercise
book iconography—shaded and sculpted by
hundreds of tiny, meticulous pen strokes.
Pointillism by way of avoiding maths homework.
Next to your face, Marcel, is printed a poem.
It is titled 'Armoury Show', and it is written
by Scottish writer-cum-dandy-cum-musician-
cum-model-cum-TV-presenter Richard Jobson,
who also reads the poem on track 11 of the
album.

Note: The sleeve to 'From Brussels with
Love' uses the English spelling of Armoury
A.R.M.O.U.R.Y. rather than the shorter
Americanized spelling A.R.M.O.R.Y.
I wonder what this signifies. COMPRESSION?
EXPANSION? EFFICIENCY? Let's add them
to the vocab list anyway.

"ARMOURY SHOW"

"ARMOURY SHOW
To be popular, one must be a mediocrity
Paschally polished window panes
Refracted light through Armoury Show
Oh Armoury Show
The solution and the problem
Oh Armoury Show
The solution kills the problem
Oh Armoury Show
Armoury Show
Die macht der musik
Oh crazy vorld, you blessed freak show
Is it true I rejoice
Over every dead German?
Perception of realism the banner
Unrelative, unrelative,
Unrelative, unrelative
A hypocrite in pleasure
Never, never, never!
Oh Armoury Show
Somebody must have the last word
The symposium of sycophants
Tell that simple is not best
But best is always simple
ART IS DEAD
LONG LIVE THE NEW MACHINE ART
Tatlin
ART IS DEAD

Long live the new machine art. And long live
the new machine music too. Because, counter to
Theodor Adorno's miserable prediction that the
adaptation to machine music would result in a
renunciation of one's own human feelings, the
machines have made our hearts sing: just not
necessarily songs of peace, love and happiness.
Comparisons could easily be made between
'From Brussels with Love' and the Cold-War
romanticism of David Bowie's late-1970s trilogy
of albums recorded with Brian Eno in Berlin—
'Low', '"Heroes"' and 'Lodger'—records featuring
wintry electronic atmospheres bearing titles
such as 'Art Decade', 'V-2 Schneider', 'Neuköln'
and 'Warszawa'.

As the record label name Disques du Crépuscule
suggests, 'From Brussels with Love' is a twilight
album. Bookended with two icy synthesizer
sketches by Ultravox's John Foxx, almost
every one of the 20 tracks on the album is an
unabashedly melancholy paean to life in a post-
war, social democratic Europe. It also includes
two interviews: one with intellectual pop aesthete
Brian Eno, and one with iconic French actress
Jeanne Moreau, in French, untranslated, and to
the accompaniment of Erik Satie compositions
for piano. According to Crépuscule archivist
James Nice, interviews with Marguerite Duras,
Michel Tournier and Alan Robbe-Grillet were
also on the wish-list. The second track on the
album is 'Airwaves' recorded by Thomas Dolby.
The song locates the album somewhere between
Berlin and New York. The sound of a radio
tunes in and out. Dolby—sounding more Bowie
than the Man Who Fell To Earth himself—
plays the Old World European lost in the
electric New World of Brooklyn and Manhattan.
The song's lyrics are peppered with words
such as BROADCAST, ANTENNA, CABLE, WIRE,
PYLON and MOTOR HOMES. 'Airwaves' is
pure Modernist nostalgia—an ode to all that
post-war Modernism promised us—25 years
before it became fashionable.

David Bowie, WARSZAWA

Thomas Dolby, AIRWAVES
"Strange how the scale forms
In tiny patterns
On my antenna
And the 5 o'clock Show,
hello, hello ...
Brooklyn is crawling
With famous people

65

I turn my vehicle
Beneath the river west from south ..."

By way of contrast, the album doesn't flinch from alienation and aggression either. Post-punk austerity is fused with Dadaist pranksterism in the form of tracks by bands such as Repetition, Radio Romance, Der Plan, The Names and Wire's Graham Lewis and B.C. Gilbert—jarring, stabbing guitars, rusting drum machines, multilingual lyrics and not an American accent to be heard anywhere.

Repetition, STRANGER
Radio Romance, ÉTRANGE AFFINITÉ
Plan, MEINE FRUENDE
Lewis & Gilbert, TWIST UP

Where these tracks are characterized by electric-metallic astringency or agit-prop playfulness —suggesting angry political dissidents, or communities of squatters eking an existence in the bombed-out edges of a city—elsewhere there is a pervasive sense of resignation. It can be heard in the Durutti Column's 'Sleep Will Come' or the song 'Haystack'—Kevin Hewick & New Order's clunky but affecting description of a relationship played out through heroin addiction. 'Haystack' was the first time the ex-Joy Division members had played since the suicide of the band's singer Ian Curtis. Twenty-seven years later, Curtis would be canonized by a major motion picture dramatization of his life and, as writer Michael Bracewell observes, become to contemporary artists in 2008 what daffodils were to Wordsworth. Add his name to the vocab list, somewhere between the words RADIO and TRANSMISSION.

Duritti Column, SLEEP WILL COME
Kevin Newick & New Order, HAYSTACK

'From Brussels with Love' also features four pieces by musicians with feet in the world of modern composition rather than post-punk angst. 'A Walk Through H (Reincarnation of an Ornithologist)' is by Michael Nyman, the critic-turned-composer who first applied the term 'Minimalism' to music. This piece was originally written for Peter Greenaway's film 'A Walk Through H', and its charmingly wheezy strings chug along like an unhealthy Philip Glass out jogging. Phil Niblock's 'A Third Trombone' provides languid backing drones to the Brian Eno interview. Harold Budd's 'Children on the Hill' and Gavin Bryars' gently breathtaking 'White's SS' are vividly crepuscular; Minimalist piano melodies that sound like they're played in empty drawing-rooms at dusk, the music's only listeners being dust motes dancing in the fading light.

66

Bryars' piece took its title from an approach to making music used by his friend John White. The 'SS' acronym does not allude directly to the Third Reich—although you'd be forgiven for thinking this in the Euro-historical atmosphere of 'From Brussels with Love'—rather, it stands for 'systems and sentimentality'. How apt!

Weren't you, Marcel, the first Romantic Conceptualist artist, with your hidden artworks, mysterious bachelors and years spent playing chess, spent playing things so straight and deadpan it became weird? OH ARMOURY SHOW!

These classically-influenced tracks speak not of punk but of high culture—of music that reaches back into the past: the heroic age of modern composition; summers spent in Darmstadt debating New Music with Pierre Boulez and Karlheinz Stockhausen, the youthful American minimalism of Steve Reich and Philip Glass. These are 'From Brussels with Love''s musical equivalent of a serif font or the photograph of a classical statue that appears on the album's sleeve. Designed by Benoit Hennebert, with Jean-François Octave and Claude Stassart, the sleeve features texts in French, Russian, English, Japanese and German, illustrated with Octave's pen-and-ink drawings. These depict a hooded figure on the shore of a lake, empty armchairs in a wood-panelled room looking out onto alpine landscapes, a lonely bed-sit and that hand-drawn portrait of Duchamp—a face mask readymade to aid short-cut dalliances with the stylistic romance of MittelEuropan intellectualism, of exiles from old Europe helping forge the culture of Young America. It is a pop appropriation of art history that fellow artist Peter Saville had understood with his contemporaneous designs for Factory Records. Living in Manchester in the late 1970s, the atmospheres evoked by European Modernist aesthetics seemed both a world apart from the grim, post-industrial realities of North West England, and also strangely similar. If you were of a romantic enough disposition, and half closed your eyes as you trudged through the rainy streets of 1970s Manchester, you could imagine yourself in 1970s Berlin—the kind of city where the stakes are high: a place for existential crises, espionage and experimental rock. A battlefield for global ideologies.

OH ARMOURY SHOW!

Oh crazy world, you blessed freak show. This appropriation of European avant-garde imagery was another take on the age-old strategy 67 of using art, music and fashion as a way to dream your way out of a bad situation. In a 1976 essay for 'Harpers & Queen', Peter York identified a particular fashion tribe that would exemplify this: the peculiars and exquisites he collectively described as Them. Them were culture-savvy connoisseurs of Pop Art Fashion, proto-New Romantic products of the 1960s art school bulge and the mainstream assimilation of camp. Thems could turn your head in the street with their sense of fashion and poise, collaging together; Chinoiserie fabrics and Eileen Gray furniture, kitsch 1950s pop trash and Clarice Cliff ceramics. Thems lived art, demonstrating astonishing levels of design literacy. Thems loved: Schiaparelli, Warhol, Rose Sélavy, Cathy McGowan, Cocteau, Marcel Duchamp, John Stefanidis, Zandra Rhodes and Ossie Clark. Thems listened to Roxy Music, David Bowie, Lou Reed and the Sex Pistols. Thems hated Kenneth Noland, Led Zeppelin, hippies, Hermann Hesse, Kris Kristofferson and J.R.R. Tolkein. Favourite Them song lines were: "Looks, looks, looks"—Sparks; "You're still doing things I gave up years ago"—Lou Reed; "Andy Warhol, silver screen, can't tell 'em apart at all"—Bowie; and "New York, New York, it's a wonderful town", as rendered by Little Nell Campbell.

And then came the sobering smack in the face of punk. The aesthetic of 'From Brussels with Love' was that of Thems left standing amidst broken glass and rubble, the party over. It was the sound of fashion and pop chastened by punk's violence, retreating into libraries and art history books, before emerging again as peacock New Romanticism (taking with it all post-punk's referencing of European history: the Blitz club, Berlin cabaret). Traditionally, youth subcultures never expect to get old. Yet the children of Crépuscule wanted to be old; old in terms of heritage, cultural capital and artistic gravitas but young in terms of looks—its image constructed from photographs of brave avant-garde pioneers in the 1920s, or beautifully damaged hangers-on at Warhol's Factory. This was pop—which had lived for so long according to the clichéd creed of youth, newness and disposability, realizing that history—in this case that of Modernism—might have something to say.

The strategy of imagining a new career in a new town through art, music and fashion hasn't gone away. If you were to draw a picture of an archetypal 'From Brussels with Love' listener, inked in black in the margins of some second-hand copy of the album picked up today, there would be little difference between the 1980 and 2008 versions. They would be young women

68

dressed like Jeanne Moreau in 'Jules et Jim', hanging out in grim new-build towns with forlorn young men in long trenchcoats and 1940s-go-1980s haircuts. On the one hand they would be nostalgic for a postwar Europe of faded grandeur, and intellectuals living in exile from a Cold War never experienced first-hand, for cafés filled with radical intellectuals and doomed lovers on the overnight Trans-Europe Express to Vienna, fantasies fuelled by YouTube clips of Bowie singing 'Heroes' in German—"Dann sind wir helden, Nur diesen tag ..."—and Kraftwerk pretending to be robots. On the other hand they would be aware that a wonderful "intelligent dilettantism" might just be their ticket out of there. A bit of what York termed "antique modern fun". Remember, the slang's simple: RADIO, CABLE, BERLIN, TELEX ...

'UN ENTRETIEN AVÉC JEANNE MOREAU' PLAYS THROUGH THE RIGHT SPEAKER ON LOW VOLUME, WITH SIMULTANEOUS TRANSLATION BY SARAH CROWNER IN THE LEFT SPEAKER READ BY SARA LE TURCQ AT HIGH VOLUME:

Erik Satie, VARIOUS ▸━━━ ◦◦◦◦◦━━◦◦◦◦◦◦ ◦

"A very difficult life in Paris with my mother, who was English, and had almost been imprisoned by the Germans. My father was on the other side of the demarcation line ... But at the same time, there existed an extraordinary relief because there was so much anarchy—without a regular sense of authority and for me it was very, very amusing ...

The character of Simone Signoret was based on a cousin of mine who lived in Le Puy de Dôme. And she was a woman who really taught me so much. She made me profoundly happy because my parents, who ran a restaurant, had very little time to take care of me. And, with her I discovered the virtue of hard work, the power of nature, all the mysteries of a ... of a deep life ... not an adulterated life, do you know what I mean?

She was a woman who was very strong but at the same time very sweet, very much a believer in a kind of divine law. So she believed in equality for everyone.

Cinema gives me as much as I have given to it.

I like good people, whether they are male or female. I don't like idiots whether they are male or female.

A friend?—ah!—I'm gonna give it to her ... !

I think one must know how to be able to use anything. To be able to understand everything, the whys of things, failures, successes ...

I will soon play in a film by George

"Une vie très difficile à Paris avec ma mère qui était anglaise, qui a failli être imprisioner pas les allemands. Mon père qui était de l'autre coté de la ligne de démarcation ... Mais au meme temps un soulagement extraordinaire parce qu'il y avait une vraie anarchie, il n'y a plus d'autorité habituelle et c'était vraiment très amusant ...

Pour le personnage de Simone Signoret est une lointaine cousine qui vivait dans le Puy de Dôme. Et, c'est une femme qui m'a beaucoup appris. Et avec laquelle j'étais profondement heureuse parce que mes parents qui étaient hoteliers- restaurateurs, et avaient peu de temps s'occuper a moi. Et a travers elle, j'ai decouverte la vertu du travail, la force de la nature, tous les mystères de la ... de la vie profonde, de la vie ... pas la vie frelater, voyez ce que je veux dire?

C'était une femme très forte et au meme temps très douce, très très croyante dans les lois divine, donc elle croyait un autre égalite a tous.

Le cinema m'apporte autant que je lui apporter.

J'aime les gens bien, qu'il soit masculin ou feminine, et je n'aime pas les cons qu'il soit masculin ou feminine.

Une amie—ah—Je vais lui donner ... !

Je pense qu'il faut savoir de servir de tout. De savoir comprendre tout. Et les pourquois des choses, les échecs, les succès ...

Je vais tourner comme comedienne, la, dans un film de George Katzander, avec Marie-France Pisier, des acteurs américains, un film sur

69

Katzander, with Marie France Pisier and American actors, about Coco Chanel. I am also preparing some songs that I will record as several LPs, based on magnificent works by a Belgian poet, called Norge.

The most commercial films I've made were 'Les Amants', 'Diary of a Chambermaid', and 'Ascenceur pour l'Echafaud'. 'Viva Maria!' didn't bring the success we expected at all. 'Mata-Hari' was not a triumph ... We had to go to court, and had a trial. We didn't even distribute it in the United States. People never saw it.

I regret nothing! I have better things to do than to look back thinking of the past, telling myself shit about this or that.

The seven wonders of the world? Do you want me to put them in order? Man is a wonder, the plants are a wonder, the animals are a wonder ... the elements, another wonder, that makes four ... the wind, which we don't see, that's a wonder ... the sky, the stars ... wonders ...

Well, politics bores me! I think it is a puppet show, completely ridiculous. I watch these men on the TV and I find them bad, with bad make-up, they're ugly. Political life wears down people so quickly, it's extraordinary.

I think about life and death ... yes ... I try to use time the best as I can.

Intellectualism, its like a language, a construction, a quibble, these certain critical discourses. But intelligence is something original, that has a liveliness which comes from true, sincere ... right ... thoughts.

I think that beauty is what emanates from within ... a radiance ... the interior life."

Coco Chanel. Et puis, je prépare des chansons que je vais enregistrer, pour faire plusieurs 33 tours, d'après les oeuvres magnifiques d'un poète d'origine Belge, qui s'appelle Norge.

Les films les plus commerciaux ca été 'Les Amants', 'c'était Journal d' une Femme de Chambre', ça été 'Ascenseur Pour l'Echau-faux'.'Viva Maria!' n'a pas porter les fruits que l'on a attendé. 'Mata-Hari' n'a pas était un tri-omphe ... On a eu un process. On a même pas pu l'éxploiter aux Etats-Unis. Les gens n'ont pas vus.

Je ne regrette rien! J'ai les choses a faire, que de penser au passé, en me disant ... de penser ceci cela.

Les sept merveilles du monde? Voulez-vous que je fasse un numération? L'air est un merveille, la végétation est un merveille, les animaux sont une merveille, les éléments, un autre merveille, ca fait quatre ... le vent qu'on voit pas, c'est une merveille ... le ciel, les étoiles ... une merveille.

Moi, la politique ça m'emmerde! Je trouve que c'est un guignol, complètement ridicule. Je regarde ces mecs a la télé, je trouve qu'il sont mauvais, ils sont mal maquillées, ils sont moches. La vie politique abime les hommes avec une rapidité absoluement extraordinaire.

Je pense a la vie et a la mort ... oui ... J'essaie de bien employer mon temps.

Intellectuel, c'est comme un language, c'est un construction c'est un rationalisation, ces certains discours critique. Mais l'intelligence c'est quelque chose qui est original, qui a de la vivacité, qui naît de la vraies pensées ... sincères ... et justes.

Je pense que la beauté ce qui emane ... c'est la radiation ... c'est la vie interieur."

BACK TO PREVIOUS FORMAT. DAN FOX IN LEFT CHANNEL.

Paul Morley, reviewing 'From Brussels with Love' for the 'NME' in 1980, wrote: "Of course it's posey: what isn't? It's pop/art. Insufferably over-fashionable, lavishly over the top, dreadfully, dilletantish, finely eclectic. Pop can be so many things."

Trivia fact: Morley himself was later to be in a band named The Art of Noise, after an essay on music by Futurist Luigi Rossolo. He also started a label called Zang Tumb Tumb, in homage to a poem by Filippo Tommasso Marinetti.

Track nine of the compilation—just before Jeanne Moreau—is the interview with Eno.

Phil Niblock, A THIRD TROMBONE ———
"For me the great strength of dilettantism is that it tends to come in from another angle.

It doesn't always, of course. The other way of being a dilettante is just by doing the most pedantic and obvious things. But an intelligent dilettante will not be constrained by the limitations of what's normally considered possible. He won't be frightened, he's got nothing to lose. You know, a person who has his career at stake on every piece of work is obviously going to be a bit more defensive about what he does, whereas the dilettante who just kind of says, oh, I'll try this for a while, is not so frightened of failure, I would imagine. But to maintain a dilettante attitude consciously is also rather suspicious. I guess I'm past the dilettante phase now [laughs]. I've decided that I AM a musician or composer, and that's what I do. And I generally can't pretend to be naïve anymore, though I'm still musically naïve, in a sense. I have to take a different approach now to what I'm doing.

In popular arts the question of tradition is very interesting because most popular work is about 94% tradition and about 6% innovation, and that seems to me like a good kind of ratio as well. I believe that the function of culture that is always overlooked by people who are into the avant-garde and experimental music is not only to innovate but to keep rehearsing and rehashing what exists already. And rock music is a great example of this, you know, there's always … things are always being recalled and built back into the structure again. And of course what you choose to ignore and what you choose to re-enhance, to use again, is just as important a statement as the innovations you make."

Here, the key idea raised by Eno in the interview is that of "intelligent dilletantism"—the notion that pretending, and thus pretentiousness, is somehow fruitful. Some years later Eno wrote that 'The common assumption is that there are real people and there are others who are pretending to be something they're not. There is also an assumption that there's something morally wrong with pretending, My assumptions about culture as a place where you can take psychological risks without incurring physical penalities make me think that pretending is the most important thing we do. It's the way we make our thought experiments, find out what it would be like to be otherwise."

A year after 'From Brussels with Love' came out, Eno and Talking Heads frontman David Byrne released 'My Life in the Bush of Ghosts'—its cover designed by Peter Saville. Eno arrived in New York in the late 1970s fascinated by its music scene. In addition to producing the 1978 compilation 'No New York' **71**

—a snapshot of the city's No Wave bands—he worked with Talking Heads on their albums 'More Songs about Buildings and Food', 'Fear of Music' and 'Remain in Light'. Talking Heads were masters of deadpan: their preppy clothes, neat haircuts and songs about buildings, animals and government bureaucrats were so ultra-straight they were ultra-weird. During this time Eno and Byrne had struck up a close friendship and had begun to develop the ideas that would be manifested in 'My Life in the Bush of Ghosts'. Some would say this relationship was so close that they had started imitating each other's dress sense and mannerisms. According to Tina Weymouth, "by the time they finished working together for three months"—on 'Bush of Ghosts'—"they were dressing like one another … They're like two fourteen-year-old boys making an impression on each other."

Unrelative, unrelative, unrelative. A hypocrite in pleasure, never.
OH ARMOURY SHOW! … also the name of Richard Jobson's short-lived band. Here we go along that radio dial again: a spittle-spray of high-frequency chatter, a whine, a fizz and then

The Armoury Show, WAITING FOR THE FLOOD, 1984.

Talking Heads, PSYCHO KILLER, 1977. Trivia fact: Did you know that Talking Heads bass player Tina Weymouth is half-FRENCH? Pop can be so many things. OH ARMOURY SHOW!

"In Britain or Europe radio presenters are picked for their qualities of calmness and obvious rationality," said Eno to the 'Guardian' newspaper just before 'My Life in the Bush of Ghosts' was released. "Here"—in America— "you get the nuttiest people in charge of the airwaves." Featuring voices gleaned from the radio, 'My Life in the Bush of Ghosts' is a sample-heavy work of speculative fiction, originally conceived as a fake ethnographic document, the airwave flotsam and jetsam of an imaginary tribe. It is an album on which, as Morley wrote in 2005, Eno and Byrne "wondered what it would be like if Pop music had not been so American, or so European": an interesting angle on a piece of work made by an ineffably European product of art school—one who in many public interviews disavowed, like Duchamp, the importance of skill, or hands-on artistic facture—and an ineffably American product of art school whose sensibility was wrought by the downtown scene

Talking Heads, SEEN & NOT SEEN

"FA FA FA FAH FAH …"

"Fa-fa-fa fah fa-fa-fa-fa fah far better …"

of late 1970s New York. Morley argues that 'My Life in the Bush of Ghosts' is the third part of a Talking Heads trilogy—'Fear of Music', 'Remain in Light' and 'My Life in the Bush of Ghosts'. And not only that, but it is the third part of a Roxy Music trilogy—'Roxy Music', 'For Your Pleasure' and 'My Life in The Bush of Ghosts'.

Roxy Music, FOR YOUR PLEASURE
Talking Heads, HOUSES IN MOTION
Eno & Byrne, AMERICA IS WAITING

As writer Sam Thorne has observed, 'My Life in the Bush of Ghosts' has recently become another Ur-text for hipster pop. It is being transmitted prime-time once again in a logical radio dial shift across from last year's fascination with all things Factory, and the year-before-that's obsession with The Clash, and the year-before-the-year-before that with its skinny eyes on next year's yesteryear retailoring of worn, grubby velvet undergrounds. Some white light, returned with thanks.

Velvet Underground producer Tom Wilson once said that the hard-panned stereo left and right effect on the band's track 'The Gift'—in which the sonorously Welsh-accented John Cale recites Lou Reed's horror story of divorce and the U.S. Postal Service in one ear, as the band grinds on in the other—was done because he and the band had "got stereo pre-frontal lobes". The effect allows the listener, using the balance control on their stereo, to listen to one or the other, or both.

The Velvet Underground, THE GIFT
"Waldo Jeffers had reached his limit. It was now mid-August which meant he had been separated from Marsha for more than two months. Two months, and all he had to show was three dog-eared letters and two very expensive long-distance phone calls. True, when school had ended and she'd returned to Wisconsin, and he to Locust, Pennsylvania, she had sworn to maintain a certain fidelity. She would date occasionally, but merely as amusement. She would remain faithful.

But lately Waldo had begun to worry. He had trouble sleeping at night and when he did, he had horrible dreams. He lay awake at night, tossing and turning underneath his pleated quilt protector, tears welling in his eyes as he pictured Marsha, her sworn vows overcome by liquor and the smooth soothings of some neanderthal, finally submitting to the final caresses of sexual oblivion. It was more than the human mind could bear.

Visions of Marsha's faithlessness haunted him. Daytime fantasies of sexual abandon

73

permeated his thoughts. And the thing was, they wouldn't understand how she really was. He, Waldo, alone understood this. He had intuitively grasped every nook and cranny of her psyche. He had made her smile. She needed him, and he wasn't there. (Awww…)"

A song split left and right. Left for John Cale, for literature and old Europe. Right for America and the metal machine music. Art in stereo. A later track by the band, entitled 'The Murder Mystery', repeated the same trick, this time with two vocal tracks rather than just one, both speaking and singing simultaneously.

Trivia fact: The lyrics to the song were published in issue 52, Winter 1972, of 'The Paris Review'. OH MARCEL! OH ANDY! OH BRIAN! OH DAVID! OH ARMOURY SHOW!

Transatlantic stereo pre-frontal lobes. Europe, America, Andy Warhol, the Velvet Underground, Roxy, Eno, Byrne, Crépuscule, Talking Heads, New York old wave, New York New Wave, New York No Wave. Like the romanticized Euro-Modernist existentialism evoked on 'From Brussels with Love', are these not also ciphers? A short-cut means of describing an "insufferably over-fashionable, lavishly over the top, dreadfully, dilletantish, finely eclectic" shot aimed right between the eyes of art and pop? A detour that cuts across Rockist myths of bluesy authenticity and folkster earnestness, and instead heads in hot pursuit of Art?

The Velvet Underground, I'LL BE YOUR MIRROR

A third, and sometimes overlooked, contributor to the ideas behind 'My Life in the Bush of Ghosts', is composer Jon Hassell, whose album 'Vernal Equinox' was released three years before 'From Brussels with Love'. At the time, Hassell had been advancing his concept of what he called Fourth World music: "A proposal for a 'coffee-coloured' classical music of the future—both in terms of the adoption of entirely new modes of structural organization (as might be suggested by the computer ability to re-arrange, dot-by-dot, a sound or video image) and in terms of an expansion of the 'allowable' musical vocabulary in which one may speak this structure—leaving behind the ascetic face which Eurocentric tradition has come to associate with serious expression."

Pop remains in refracted light through armoury show: it always puts on its ascetic face—monochrome minimal/classical romantic austerity—when it wants to be believed in as Art with a capital 'A'. Pop music theatricalizes art's post-war aesthetic and conceptual problems—those of the authorial voice, the readymade, performance, gender, politics, the market, and now, in the digital present, the infinitely downloadable, dematerialized object of the recorded song.

Back along that radio dial again, back east to Brussels by way of Manchester, south a few degrees to 1980.

'From Brussels with Love' had a sleeper agent in its midst. It was a song that appeared on the album's first release, but disappeared from released versions, encouraged to resign "for reasons of space". 'Felch' by A Certain Ratio is the album's secret American disco connection.

A Certain Ratio were on Factory Records, label-mates with the fragile Durutti Column and doomed Joy Division, but this lewdly-titled punk funk outburst is the only dancefloor moment on 'From Brussels with Love'. A Certain Ratio dressed like colonial soldiers on postings to hot Middle-Eastern territories: khaki shorts, neat, functional 1940s haircuts. Their guitars, keyboards and klaxon-like trumpets were as abrasive as any punk band's, but their sound was funk to the core. 'Felch''s inclusion on 'From Brussels with Love' speaks to the links between Berlin-era Bowie, Kraftwerk and the U.S. disco scene. Bowie's Berlin albums were nothing if not the sound of the advance guard of disco. The story goes that one day, during the recording of Bowie's album 'Low', Eno heard a record being played in a Berlin record store and was so taken by it he immediately bought a copy and rushed back to the studio, declaring it to be "the future of music". The record was 'I Feel Love' by Donna Summer. Kraftwerk's machine pulse hymns to Deutsche Bank, Interpol, trains, planes and computers—to Common Market efficiency and productivity—were a huge influence on disco. It was music so stiff it was funky. One Manhattan record shop employee remarked to the 'Village Voice' in the late 1970s that "Typically, I'll sell Kraftwerk's 'Trans-Europe Express' to a fourteen year-old back kid carrying a stick and a giant radio." As journalist Nelson George wrote, "music with a metronome-like beat—perfect for folks with no sense of rhythm—almost inflectionless vocals, and metallic sexuality matched the high-tech, high-sex, and low-passion atmosphere of the glamorous discos that appeared in every major American city." 'From Brussels with Love' was the existential sound of a new dawn fading, but was that because it was dawn seen whilst stumbling out of a Brussels Eurodisco, after a night of cocktails with

John Hassell, HEX

A Certain Ratio, FELCH

75

businessmen from Frankfurt? Was it the twilight prelude to a lost weekend with arch-Thems Andy, Grace and Bianca at Studio 54?

Joe Strummer of The Clash said that David Bowie "makes decadent disco music" and that "it sure ain't rock'n'roll". So what? Johnny Rotten was never embarrassed about loving reggae and disco. Who needs rock'n'roll when you have Grace Jones making the children of Crépuscule smile with dub-disco cover versions of Roxy Music's 'Love is the Drug' and Joy Division's 'She's Lost Control'? UK art school grads and gloomy post-punk bands alike were always welcome dancefloor guests.

Back across the sea to New York. Eno and Byrne's pop-intellectual romance forms mirror images of Europhilic American music and Americo-philic European art. And as pop continues to chase its own tail today, 'My Life in the Bush of Ghosts' arrives with us From Santiago-Tokyo-Lagos with Love. For all its claims to a more holistic, globalized approach to music, it remains an undeniably Anglo-American sounding album. As Jerome Davis said of Talking Heads, it is "a white, Quaker-Scottish-British-French-Harvard-Kentuckian version of African music." World Music in exile, reified and ratified by post-Punk. Factory and Crépuscule Records returning home with tanned, weather-beaten skin, speaking Swahili or Mandarin rather than German or French—other ways of saying the same things, of keeping on the same trajectories. It is, like 'From Brussels with Love', a collection of atmospheres—content residing not in the recording itself so much as in the dust between your hi-fi speaker and your imagination. The 'Bush of Ghosts' look in 2008 is still easy, but also markedly similar to the look of 'From Brussels with Love' 2008—perhaps a little more preppy, button-down, a short back and sides for the men and an Edie Sedgwick crop for the women—that grey overcoat perhaps accessorized by an Arab keffiyeh from Urban Outfitters, or a brightly coloured T-shirt from American Apparel. Good looking, culture-savvy and impeccably eccentric in a Wes Anderson film kinda way. And the vocab's much the same, just a touch more ekphratically exotic: RADIO, TELEX, CABLE—sure, but what about REGGAETON, AFRO-BEAT, TROPICALISMO, MIDDLE-EASTERN-PSYCH-GOSPEL, FELA KUTI, CZECH-POLISH-UKRAINIAN CONCEPTUALISM, CAPE COD KWASSA-KWASSA ...

Kraftwerk, TRANS-EUROPE EXPRESS
Donna Summer, I FEEL LOVE

Grace Jones, SHE'S LOST CONTROL

76

It's Modernist nostalgia in the age of
Easyjet flights and global warming. This year's
favourite American bands—Vampire Weekend,
Yeasayer or Gang Gang Dance—are popular
in Europe not just because of their downtown,
artsy credentials, but because they restage
that Talking Heads blueprint of "a white,
Quaker-Scottish-British-French-Harvard-
Kentuckian version" of the rest of the world's
music. They look like a European's idea of
wealthy, progressive, Hamptons-holidaying,
biennale-hopping American Thems. Just add
to your list of destinations, somewhere
between Neuköln and Brussels, Sao Paulo,
Lagos and Beijing. Even the political climate
of the early 21st century is much the same.
As Peter York put it: "fragmentation, devolution,
fantasy and paranoia—impossible new
situations like Stagflation, the Arabs, oil money
and political power ... the property market
and secondary bank collapse." The world
expands. The world contracts. OH ARMOURY
SHOW!

Strange how the scale forms ... in tiny patterns
... on my antenna ... and the 5 o' clock show,
hello, hello ... Old Wave, New Wave, long wave,
short wave. Left or right? New York or Paris?
"The solution kills the problem." But Marcel,
didn't you also hold that "There is no solution
because there is no problem"? Light pours
out of the radio. Refracted light through armory
show.
  OH ARMOURY SHOW!
  ARMOURY SHOW.
  ARMOURY SHOW.

Vampire Weekend, CAPE COD KWASSA
KWASSA

Thomas Dolby, AIRWAVES
"Be in my broadcast
When this is over
Give me your shoulder
I need a place to wait for morning
No it was nothing
Some car backfiring
Please don't ask questions
I itch all over, let me sleep
Through the airwaves
People never read the airwaves
Do we only feed the airwaves
Or stamp them out at street level?
Airwaves
The dampness of the wind
The airwaves
The tension of the skin
The airwaves
I really should have seen
Through the airwaves ..."

77

AS THE SONG FADES, THE SPOTLIGHTS COME BACK ON TO SIGNAL THE FIRST INTERMISSION OF THE EVENING. DURING THIS BREAK THE FOLLOWING TEXT IS PROJECTED ONTO THE CURTAIN, WHICH RIPPLES GENTLY.

CARNIVAL THEORY (A PLAY IN PROGRESS) by Jennifer Higgie

IT WOULD BE EXTREMELY INTERESTING TO WRITE THE HISTORY OF LAUGHTER. (Alexander Herzen)

CARNIVAL: "Time of merrymaking before lent" from It. CARNEVALE "Shrove Tuesday" from older It. forms like Milanese CARNELEVALE, O. Pisan CARNELEVARE "to remove meat" lit. "raising flesh" from L. CARO "flesh" + LEVARE "lighten, raise" folk etymology is from M.L. CARNE VALE: "flesh, farewell"

CARNIVAL THEORY explores the gulf between the internal worlds of two people contrasted with the physical world they move through. Their conversation is tempered by the problems of inhabiting, translating and responding to the world in a fresh way while being worn down by its everyday logic.

THE CARNIVAL OFFERS THE CHANCE TO HAVE A NEW OUTLOOK ON THE WORLD, TO REALIZE THE RELATIVE NATURE OF ALL THAT EXISTS, AND TO ENTER A COMPLETELY NEW ORDER OF THINGS. (Mikhail Bakhtin)

ROUGH DRAFT: How attempts at intimacy, or translating an inner world into the outer world, usually fails on some level, but we persist with it anyway (or be lonely, otherwise) = About the mysterious solace of objects and animals = Dialogue to descend into a space in which the line between thinking and speaking becomes unclear = To embody something rather than explain it.

LEHRSTÜCK (after Bertolt Brecht): Teaches by being played, not by being watched, where the purpose of a play, more than entertainment or the imitation of reality, is to present ideas = Characters are not intended to mimic real people, but to represent opposing sides of an argument, archetypes, or stereotypes = The audience should always be aware that it is watching a play = Brecht described this ideal as the VERFREMDUNGSEFFEKT, which is variously translated as 'Alienation effect', 'Defamiliarization effect', 'Distancing effect', or 'Estrangement effect'. It is the opposite of the suspension of disbelief (a situation I find impossible).

Set and costumes to be designed by Donna Huddleston and David Noonan.

Excerpts: Scenes 1, 2, 3 and 7

I MEANT TO WRITE ABOUT DEATH, ONLY LIFE CAME BREAKING IN, AS USUAL. (Virginia Woolf)

BY NOW THE AUDIENCE IS REASSEMBLED. A MAN AND A WOMAN, NEITHER YOUNG NOR OLD, WALK OUT IN FRONT OF THE CURTAIN. THE MAN STANDS BEHIND THE LEFT LECTERN, THE WOMAN BEHIND THE RIGHT LECTERN.

BEHIND AND ABOVE THEM THE TEXT IS REPLACED BY THE FIRST IN A SLOW SEQUENCE OF IMAGES SELECTED IN RESPONSE TO THE SCRIPT BY DONNA HUDDLESTON AND DAVID NOONAN. THE MAN AND WOMAN BEGIN TO READ FROM THE FOLLOWING SCRIPT. IN ADDITION TO HER OWN HALF OF THE DIALOGUE, THE WOMAN ALSO READS ALL INTRODUCTORY SCENARIOS.

TUDOR STYLE (David Noonan, 2004)

79

SCENE 1. MAN and WOMAN sit in a room. They are in very elaborate fancy dress, as if about to go to a party, but they are not festive. The WOMAN is dressed a little like Marie Antoinette, the man like Noel Coward in his youth, in a top hat and evening dress.

WOMAN: What?

MAN: I'm not looking forward to this. [Beat] When does it begin?

WOMAN: I've told you.

MAN: Remind me?

WOMAN: When the others arrive.

MAN: I hate fancy dress.

WOMAN: It suits you.

MAN: You look insane.

WOMAN: So kind.

MAN: I'm too tired to even sleep.

WOMAN: Well I've been up all day.

MAN: We have only known each other for 336 hours.

WOMAN: Nearer 337.

MAN: Isn't it a little tasteless to dress up like someone who had their head chopped off?

WOMAN: Do you always accentuate the negative?

MAN: Marie-Antoinette might agree with me.

WOMAN: You don't know her.

MAN: You can talk.

WOMAN: I hardly know you.

MAN: 336 and 3/4 hours is not nothing.

WOMAN: Unless you're an ant. Or a sprinter.

MAN: Or a pedant. [Beat] I'm just not in the mood.

WOMAN: Perhaps it's best if we simply remain acquaintances.

MAN: It's such an odd thing to do, don't you think? Put on fancy dress in order to break the ice? [Beat] Nonetheless, there is something about you. [Beat] Why on earth did you invite me to this?

WOMAN: I thought you'd like it.

MAN: A carnival is not carrots.

WOMAN: It's a theory of resistance.

MAN: Of what?

WOMAN: Of the tough portal of reality.

MAN: Perhaps it's the sheer rigour and breadth of your mind that attracts me.

WOMAN: You're a man who likes order.

MAN: That sounds like a criticism.

WOMAN: You refuse to accommodate my line of thinking. That's the beginnings of fascism.

MAN: An aversion to dressing up does not make me a fascist.

WOMAN: I do apologize. I was, perhaps, extreme.

MAN: You are as melancholy as a bridge in rain.

WOMAN: Have you never enjoyed a carnival?

MAN: Only when they're dark and the wine is flowing and I am allowed to observe young beauties dance their way to oblivion.

WOMAN: Blimey.

MAN: Perhaps oblivion is too extreme a word.

WOMAN: You need a safety valve. Like all carnivals.

MAN: I will take your retort as a compliment, but I must insist, that I am by no means a carnival.

WOMAN: That you can utter such blunt truths at such short acquaintance is surely promising.

MAN: Perhaps we are soul-mates.

WOMAN: Are you always this bitter?

MAN: Not always.

WOMAN: I have learnt too many useless things. I hear my mother cough and do not know how to heal her.

MAN: You are behaving like an aristocrat. All mothers cough.

WOMAN: Perhaps I am an aristocrat.

MAN: You are not. You're just a silly woman in a silly dress.

WOMAN: True. And you are right. You are not, by any means, a carnival.

MAN: You're not alone you know.

WOMAN: I'm not so sure. Everyone is one of two. And we two are not one.

MAN: Not yet anyway.

WOMAN: Hmm.

MAN: It is important to attempt things without thoughts of failure.

WOMAN: What, being alone?

MAN: Why not?

WOMAN: You are an optimist. No. Another word.

MAN: Name it.

WOMAN: Who was it who said it is best to avoid thoughts of plumbing and death?

MAN: That is not a word. [Beat] Last night I lay on my bed so weary it occurred to me: this is no life. The curtains were open; the moon was up, dusty and fat, a full town moon. Pregnant clouds raced towards it and swallowed. One bird yelled and none replied. It began to rain; cars on the road sounded like a single giant car. Nothing had changed but I felt a little odd; as if some big decision had been made that I'm not yet aware of. I turned out the light and slept straight away. It must have been a few hours later when the window flew open and woke me up; the curtains billowed out like the sails of an ancient ship. [Beat] For god's sake, where are the others?

WOMAN: Aha! You crave the carnival!

MAN: You are driving me into its arms.

WOMAN: But it shall not make me jealous!

MAN: (Deflated) These silk pantaloons are itchy!

WOMAN: Did you mention a ship.

MAN: On second thoughts, I believe it was not a ship, despite its appearance.

WOMAN: I don't understand.

MAN: I slammed the window and slept again and dreamt of the sea; an empty, clean place the likes of which I hadn't seen for far too long.

WOMAN: And when you woke?

MAN: My eyes snapped open! I leaned out of the window and breathed; felt fresh enough to explode! The world was doing its thing, and I had spent a year not noticing it. The flowers were blooming and the wind was up. Pollen danced giddy, banged on doors; the earth gleamed ready to grow. A nice brisk pinch trembled at the edge of warmth. Possibility pounded at my door and I was getting old. Men shouted joyfully in argument while they flung their fists at jaws in celebration. Women sang as their tights laddered, kids leapt from buses, skipped to school and kissed.

WOMAN: Are you making this up?

MAN: Not a word is false. I leaned further out the window. In the distance rivers plunged over rocks as kittens swam to shore undrowned, shook the sacks from their heads and laughed. Old dogs galloped in parks and birds fell from the sky dizzy with hope.

WOMAN: How many women have you slept with?

MAN: I can't remember. So many memories encourage amnesia!

WOMAN: Too true.

MAN: And you?

WOMAN: Does kissing count?

MAN: Only as a weapon.

WOMAN: My discretion inhibits me.

MAN: Fair enough.

WOMAN: The question is always of the whys and wherefores of 'yes'.

MAN: Do you want to be yesed?

WOMAN: Not sure.

MAN: What a precipice. [Beat] When I turned back to my room the light looked startled. I stretched. My shoulders were frozen and my back was like a board. A clammy mouth. Legs strung out, fingers stiff.

WOMAN: You are almost not young.

MAN: And you are even older.

WOMAN: That is not gentlemanly.

MAN: The slumber which has snatched a year of my life is over.

WOMAN: My old Dad used to say that nothing will cheer you up more than a man singing in prison.

MAN: You can touch skin if you like.

WOMAN: I'm not an experience!

MAN: Who mentioned experience?

WOMAN: Speaking of which, I went to the hairdresser this morning and my eye was caught by an ad for a perfume called 'Mood Indigo'. A crisp silhouette of a garden, a woman's pert little profile beneath wistful hair facing a future which rolled out before her like gold leaf. The ad worked. I went and bought some.

MAN: (Sniffs) Floral and powdery with notes of aniseed, carnation, vanilla and rose.

WOMAN: Apparently, early last century on a spring evening, a young woman was overcome by intense agitation while taking the air in a fragrant garden in the South of France.

MAN: (Suddenly yelling) Morning? Night? For god's sake, can't you be more specific?

WOMAN: (Startled, yelling back) In the twilight hour when the sky has lost its sun but not yet found its stars. 'Mood Indigo': "an emotion which only this perfume can express."

MAN: You are not pert, by any stretch of the imagination.

WOMAN: Your intentions are intentionally unclear.

MAN: And you do not have a garden.

WOMAN: Very few people have gardens. I shouldn't have told you. (To herself) A lack of a garden is always such ammunition for a man.

MAN: Why do you want a garden anyway?

WOMAN: I suspect it might relieve the intense agitation of my life.

MAN: You don't seem intensely agitated.

WOMAN: Intense agitation is so normal an occurrence I do not know why I should bother to mention it.

MAN: But this is why we live in cities! We love the indifference of the multitudes!

WOMAN: You twist my words.

MAN: Why did you buy the perfume?

WOMAN: Because I tasted sudden and bitter bile in my mouth and immediately recognized its source: jealousy.

MAN: Of what? An advertisement?

WOMAN: A black hole in the universe spits out what it cannot swallow.

MAN: I am filled with a longing.

WOMAN: For what?

MAN: For home.

WOMAN: So go.

MAN: And disappoint you? Never.

WOMAN: The weather is so rarely what you expect.

81

=

SCENE 2. MAN and WOMAN are in tennis clothes holding tennis racquets.

WOMAN: (Dreamy) The hairdresser played my scalp like a virtuoso violinist plays a violin. Once the job was done, I walked down the street with my tingling, glossy head held high stalking a feeling I could not yet identify. Like long-lost acquaintances nocturnal liaisons remembered themselves to me. Flesh, ignored this past year, appealed to the higher court of my mind. A year of lonely slumber. If I didn't watch it, my body, the one that transported my soul through the messy streets of life would soon to be relegated to the dustbin of history. Skin sent me begging letters as I strode. Mind dragged flesh up from the dock it had sunk into. Flesh sighed. I bought an éclair and ate it as I walked along. It tasted good.

MAN: I am a fine lover, there is no doubt about that!

WOMAN: Nothing so sweet has passed my lips for a very long time.

MAN: My darling.

WOMAN: My hunter.

MAN: I do not hunt.

WOMAN: My caveman!

MAN: In trousers?

WOMAN: Still so literal.

MAN: Shall we play now?

WOMAN: There are no courts free. Use your eyes!

MAN: But you booked?

WOMAN: Of course.

MAN: Damn.

WOMAN: Oh lighten up.

MAN: My god you're demanding. Have you ever heard of Bergen?

WOMAN: No.

MAN: It's in Norway. It is, apparently, the wettest place on earth. People still live there despite the weather.

WOMAN: Why?

MAN: It is so difficult to move.

WOMAN: So few people know where they will be buried.

MAN: Or burnt.

WOMAN: Or left at sea, to float away.

MAN: Or devoured by animals.

WOMAN: Or left on a hill, and turned to dust.

MAN: Or blown from a spacecraft and doomed to float through the universe for all eternity. [Beat] In Bergen cans of rain are sold as souvenirs in tourist shops. Once it rained for 86 days in a row. Various townspeople were interviewed beneath low grey skies.

WOMAN: How did they seem?

MAN: Cheerful.

WOMAN: How cheerful?

MAN: Like Londoners in the Blitz.

WOMAN: Ah.

MAN: Norway is good to its people, apparently.

WOMAN: But not to its whales.

MAN: No, not to its whales.

WOMAN: What an interesting place it must be. So contrary. I would like to visit the fjords. They look so clean.

MAN: Have you seen anything interesting on television lately?

WOMAN: Last night I watched a programme on near death experiences. One woman described dying as being absorbed by "a bright light in a great rush".

MAN: Goodness.

WOMAN: She said she had been living a life empty of love.

MAN: Not so unusual.

WOMAN: I didn't say it was.

MAN: Don't be defensive.

WOMAN: I'm not.

MAN: Pray continue.

WOMAN: She explained that by dying she had discovered a belief in "something divine without the need for god".

MAN: Was there a re-enactment?

WOMAN: Yes.

MAN: How did it look?

WOMAN: Like aliens emerging from a cupboard.

MAN: Is she happy now?

WOMAN: Yes. Because of dying she moved to a nice little cottage and opened a dog kennel.

MAN: What a lovely story.

WOMAN: When she talked about the dogs her eyes glittered in an odd manner.

MAN: Elaborate.

WOMAN: She was so in love with those dogs she could hardly believe it.

MAN: I cannot believe the rudeness of tennis players sometimes. They know we have booked! They know we are waiting!

WOMAN: Yes, but sometimes it's impossible to gauge the time a set takes.

MAN: (Furious) In all of the 2,232 hours we have existed uneasily side by side, do not think I have not noticed how you love to blind me with science. Do not think I haven't noticed!

WOMAN: I have never met a man less open to blinding by anything or anyone.

MAN: I watched a show on TV about a king of England. There were lots of marvellous deep red rooms bathed in peachy light.

WOMAN: Which king?

MAN: George III.

82

WOMAN: What was he famous for again?

MAN: For being "a mollusc who never found his rock". (Shouts) Why don't we ever speak about politics? Who did you vote for? Do you believe in the monarchy? I am sick to death of your fucking feelings! I don't want to manage them. Repercussions! Everything has its repercussions!

WOMAN: What on earth have I said?

MAN: Nothing! That's the point! Nothing!

WOMAN: The lover leaves, the lovee weeps. The sky drops like a collapsed ceiling, the earth turns hard and colour forgets what it was born for!

MAN: Which colour is that?

WOMAN: Convention states blue.

MAN: Like a small bud budding my sad heart trembles and my soul begins to thaw. [Beat] Do you enjoy working in the hospitality industry?

WOMAN: Hospitable is not the word.

MAN: Why are the courts not free?

WOMAN: Perhaps we cannot play.

=

SCENE 3. MAN and WOMAN are in a large bed. The blankets are pulled up high.

WOMAN: I have begun to forget things I should have remembered and held dear.

MAN: Such as?

WOMAN: I like a cold room at night and a new man in spring and vowed to my sister when I was 17 that I would not find myself, years from now in the corner of a pub, asleep beneath a rug.

MAN: A longing has erupted in you; a longing for what I couldn't say, but it is a longing nonetheless and it is as concentrated as a dog running home. [Beat] The colour of your door is like rancid butter.

WOMAN: I may as well leave town.

MAN: My body embarrasses me.

WOMAN: I do not want to know that. Embarrassment is too contagious.

MAN: I shall never mention it again.

WOMAN: But its evidence shall be everywhere.

MAN: You have no shame.

WOMAN: Shame is a shameful state.

MAN: It was raining tonight, cold mean little needles. I held my face up to the sky. It was like being kissed by a pin cushion.

WOMAN: The weather equalizes us.

MAN: I am fed up with doing sums in my head that do not add up.

WOMAN: Die in debt and you've won, my love.

MAN: Why aren't you rich?

WOMAN: It's not for want of trying.

MAN: Waitressing is not trying. [Beat] I was born very far from where I am meant to be.

WOMAN: And where is that?

MAN: You expect me to know everything.

WOMAN: All of this is a matter of timing. [Beat] What do you mean, where you are meant to be?

MAN: Did we meet in the right moment?

WOMAN: How do I know?

MAN: You just know.

WOMAN: So tell me.

MAN: It was 2,160 hours ago. It's hard to remember precisely what drew me to you.

WOMAN: You recognized me.

MAN: But I had never seen you before.

WOMAN: But nonetheless you recognized me.

MAN: I would like to die in a heroic battle.

WOMAN: There is no such thing.

MAN: I am hungry.

WOMAN: You can listen to a song and learn how to live.

MAN: Which song?

WOMAN: I can't remember the one I'm thinking of.

MAN: I am full of conservative longing.

WOMAN: For what?

MAN: A family. Money.

WOMAN: Safety should not be so fearful.

MAN: I ain't dead yet.

WOMAN: Shoot me but be sweet til you do.

MAN: I don't always know what to do with my arms when I am with you. I don't think I could bear you to see me naked.

WOMAN: No. Not yet.

MAN: But you move me.

WOMAN: I am falling apart.

=

SCENE 7. The scene looks exactly like the first scene; WOMAN and MAN are dressed in fancy dress etc. They both stare ahead.

WOMAN: Winds pushed pregnant clouds to sea, far beyond the Italian factories. On a street of pink polluted bricks we stopped to watch dull peacock wives shriek and nod as the leaves on the walls died vermilion deaths and southbound birds pierced the sky like pinholes.

MAN: I had forgotten about Italy.

WOMAN: But you must remember! In the trattoria we ate the colour white—cold grilled fish, fat beans and wine—and drank too much to talk about the things we could not say. We'll never marry here I whispered but you did not hear, drowned as you were in the

83

sound of your swallowing, your swan song,
your expectation of appropriate sound.
MAN: But I expected nothing from you!
WOMAN: Candles, sweet smells, the reverence
of singing waiters, the intimate corners.
Don't you remember? It was a church in
there, in you, around us not yet sanctified
to something unformed in dim light,
an unmarrying light, a hymn to transience.
The crowded air was introspective.
Too serious to laugh at the operatic waiter
we looked about and plied each other
with wine, and groped for visual straws, to
catalyse a subject that would fill the locks of
our conversational canal. Every subject was
paralysing, even breathing or architecture or
birds. So instead we commented on everyone
but ourselves, those murmuring, chewing
faces, distorted and soft with celestial
bruises, the ones who absorbed the light
and lines and blinked.
MAN: Beyond the ceiling a sky.
WOMAN: The dull hum of revelation split it
with secrets. Jealous, I hid and watched
them kneel and whisper in the comfortable
shadows. But still, you said, and looked at me
with eyes like mine but still you said again
and stroked my fingertips like a child.
We parted then to walk our separate ways,
if only for an hour.
MAN: An odd word to say, good-bye, a thing
beside us, a clumsy sculpture, a wrong two
words a good bye, an oxymoron carved from
anticipation.
WOMAN: I couldn't hear anyone fighting
anywhere. The roads were silent and shabby,
the dry and windy houses huddled together
like refugees from the ruins around them
as the street lights floated not far below a
fat and single sliced moon. A hill presented
itself with due gallantry so, almost together,
we rose high in the sky, and passed on the
way a small sobbing boy coming down from
something, his small face, his small hands,
clinging together for small comfort. A kissing
couple shocked me, looking as they did like
a single dark slug on a slope and it occurred
to me suddenly that both love stories and

murders begin with the discovery of a body.
MAN: From so high up, the city is no more than
a dark place scattered with shining, wet
seeds and beyond it the black oilskin sea.
All fingerprints are obliterated in time.
WOMAN: Aimless now the ascent was done,
I hummed to the sound of clouds, peered
at the unneighbourly sky, rammed hands
in pockets and jingled my change, kneeled
down and touched the dry earth, not to
join it, but to smell it. It smelt old and good.
Standing, stretching, wiping hands on my
legs the city looked about as big as a city can
get. Suddenly indifferent I knew that if your
mouth was here and wanted mine I would let
it have it for practically nothing.
MAN: You kissed him!
WOMAN: No! You're not listening! I came back
and kissed you, collapsed on a couch in a
brown and yellow room. But you did not
wake. Such a terrible distance that millimetre
of skin, between here and there, you and me.
What a strange hotel it was we had found
ourselves in. Boys laughed and tap-danced
a nervous staccato in the next room to the
accompaniment of the rhythmic, snoring man
on the other side.
MAN: It is obvious now. The sea had made
itself felt.
WOMAN: I shook a pillow. A feather floated
to the floor. You stirred and your sleeping
hands, like fingers pressed hard at the base
of an experience, begging for an eruption
snatched at air, tracing invisible portraits,
built of thumb and fingerprint and palm,
etched in the false half light of a single
bulb. You drew a sleeping shape between us,
an illustration of the wrong tale with silent,
correct lines, a prehistory of words.
MAN: Guilt, so easily ruptured and rearranged,
makes a talent of confession.
WOMAN: Before you woke, to start again,
I plucked my eyebrows to look like
birds' wings.

Blackness.

END.

THE MAN AND THE WOMAN BOW OUT TO APPLAUSE AND ANOTHER INTERMISSION.

THE AUDIENCE IS SEATED AGAIN. THE LEFT LECTERN IS NOW AT CENTRE TURNED
TO FACE OUTWARD WITH A HARDBACK BOOK ('PAPA HEMINGWAY') OPEN TO
PP. 20–21, NEXT TO A WOODEN CHAIR. S APPROACHES AND BEGINS TO SPEAK FROM
THE RIGHT LECTERN.

S : From Brussels, AGENCY is the generic name of an agency that was formed in 1992, and which constitutes an ongoing list of QUASI-THINGS, defined as items that fall just inside or outside the classifications of 'nature' and 'culture'. Specimens from the list are presented in varying assemblies, bearing witness to hesitation where those terms bifurcate. Here Agency presents the case of SPECIMEN 0880 (PAPA HEMINGWAY).

AGENCY SPEAKS FROM THE CHAIR. WHEN CALLED UPON TO DO SO, D READS CAREFULLY FROM 'PAPA HEMINGWAY'.

A : Between 1963 and 1966, A.E. Hotchner wrote a biography of the well-known writer Ernest Hemingway called 'Papa Hemingway: a personal memoir'. Hotchner met Hemingway in 1948, during the time he was writing an article about him. He became a friend, a frequent visitor to Hemingway's home and an intimate with the family. Hotchner's conversations with Hemingway, in which others sometimes also took part, included many anecdotes, memories, literary opinion and revealing comments about actual persons on whom some of Hemingway's fictional characters were based. Hotchner made careful notes of these conversations soon after they occurred. Occasionally he recorded conversations on a portable tape recorder.

During Hemingway's life Hotchner wrote and published several articles about Hemingway. After Hemingway's death on July 2, 1961 Hotchner recollected all his notes for the book 'Papa Hemingway'. The biographical study of Hemingway is chronologically limited to the period from 1948 to 1961. The style of the book is as the subtitle says: a personal memoir. Their adventures, their travels, their meetings are all described in detail. The portrait of Hemingway that emerges, is based on this particular relationship with Hotchner. Hotchner uses a conversational format wherein Hemingway is quoted extensively but always within the confines of conversations to which he was part. Woven through the narrative are lengthy quotations from Hemingway's conversations. A number of these conversational passages are reflections made by Hemingway on a wide variety of topics ranging from the personal to the literary. The last two chapters of the book are on Hemingway's final illness and suicide. Hemingway's widow is frequently mentioned in the book and is sometimes quoted. The book was published by Random House in 1966.

Ernest Hemingway wrote seven novels during his life. He received the Pulitzer Prize in 1953 for 'The Old Man and the Sea', and the Nobel Prize in Literature in 1954. Hemingway's writing style is characterized by economy and understatement. After his death in 1962

his rights were taken care of by the Estate of Hemingway and his last wife Mary Hemingway.

In 1966 Mary Hemingway sought a preliminary injunction, both on her own behalf and as executrix of Hemingway estate, in order to prohibit the forthcoming publication of 'Papa Hemingway'. Briefly, the four claims were:

1. That all of the material incorporated in the book which is based upon the language, expressions, comments and communications of Ernest Hemingway, is subject to a common law copyright, which belongs solely to his estate.

2. That the use of such material by defendants would constitute unfair competition.

3. That the book improperly incorporates material which came into the defendant author's possession while occupying a position of trust and confidence.

4. That the various references to her in the book constitute a violation of her statutory right of privacy.

The first claim concerns copyright. Mary Hemingway broadly asserted that some 65% of the contents of 'Papa Hemingway' consists of "literary matter created and expressed by Ernest Hemingway." She believed that this is subject to "common law copyright". What does that mean? A "common law copyright" could be explained as a right an author has in her unpublished literary creations. It is also often referred to as "the right of first publication".

On February 21st, 1966 a first court case ESTATE OF ERNEST HEMINGWAY & MARY HEMINGWAY VS. RANDOM HOUSE & A.E. HOTCHNER took place at the New York County Supreme Court. In his opinion, Judge Harry Frank stated:

We are thus confronted with the novel and provocative question as to whether a person's participation in spontaneous oral conversations with friends over a course of years, in distinction to lectures or prepared dialogues, may be considered a literary work subject to a common law copyright. It appears that this question of possible

85

dinner invitation was about a year ago. They served sweet champagne which he had to drink to be polite, and it took ten days for him to get it out of his system."

In early 1949, before he left for a trip to Venice, Ernest telephoned me in New York from the *finca*. He began by discussing the triumph of Mr. Truman over Mr. Dewey, but finally got to the point: "About the two stories, agreement is—deadline end of December and I deliver two stories or give back the dough, right? Wrote one story after you left but think it is too rough for *Cosmopolitan* so I better save it for the book."

"What book?"

"New book of short stories. Or book of new short stories— take your pick. Don't think I'll have time in Venice, but plan to get back to Cuba in early May, take the kids on a trip, then write two good stories for you. I may have to let them lay awhile and then go over them, but think if I have no bad luck, I should surely have two before the deadline. The story I just finished is about forty-five hundred words and much better than that Waugh crap they just ran. But I can beat it for you."

All through the spring of 1949 I received letters from Ernest from the Gritti Palace hotel in Venice and from the Villa Aprile in Cortina d'Ampezzo, which is magnificent ski country to the north. He wrote about Mary breaking her leg in a ski accident and about a serious eye infection for which he was hospitalized, but did not mention the stories. It was during this period that Ernest instigated my first meeting with Charles Scribner, Sr.; and afterward he said, "Hope you liked Charlie. He liked you very much and he likes almost nobody. Hates authors." Scribner was a silver-haired, gentle-featured man of charm, wit and good humor, and he loved Ernest as a proud father loves a gloried son. Ernest once said of Scribner: "Now that Max Perkins is gone, Charlie is all I've got left to help keep the franchise."

The first time Mr. Scribner and I met, it was to discuss Ernest's medical statement which he had sent to Scribner from Italy for release to the press. Ernest suggested that this statement might take the pressure off. "Especially off me, here in the hospital, making my fight and under siege of news hawks like Hector was be-Greeked at Troy."

The statement was: "It certainly is odd, though not particularly I suppose, for people to think you are a phony. I would not let the photographers nor any reporters in because I was too tired and was making my fight and because face was incrusted like after a flash burn. Had streptococcus infection, straphilococcus (probably misspelled) infection plus erysipelas, thirteen and one half million units of Penicillium, plus three and one half million when it started to relapse. The doctors in Cortina thought it might go into the brain and make a menengitis since the left eye was completely involved and closed completely tight so that every time I opened it with boric solution a big part of the eye-lashes would pull out.

"It could have been from the dust on the secondary roads as well as from fragments from the wad.*

"Still can't shave. Have tried it twice and up come the welts and patches and then the skin peels like postage stamps. So run a clippers over face every week. That way it looks unshaven but not as though you were sporting a beard. All above is true and accurate and you can release it to anybody, including the press."

Ernest was back in Cuba by the summer of 1949, and in late July he telephoned to report that the *Cosmopolitan* two-story project had taken another turn and suggested I visit him in September. I said that this time I would take a cottage at the Kawama Club at Varadero Beach and not inconvenience them.

"No inconvenience," Ernest said, "but Varadero beauty place. When you come down I will knock off work for two or three days and bring the boat to Varadero and we can have some fun. Will work hard for balance of July and August so that will rate the vacation."

"Arthur wants to know," I said, referring to *Cosmo*'s editor, Arthur Gordon, "if you want the additional ten thousand."

---

* Ernest is referring here to wadding fragments that fall from shotgun shells on overhead duck shots. During his hospitalization the erysipelas infected both his eyes and then spread to other parts of his face. When his eyes swelled and shut tight his doctors thought it might be fatal.

categorization of ordinary conversation as a literary work or property is one of first impression. [...]

Conversation is a media of expression of unique character. Because of its several nature any conversational exchange necessarily reflects the various participants thereto not only with respect to the direct contributions of each but also insofar as each party acts as a catalyst in evoking the thoughts and expressions of the other. The articulations of each are to some extent indelibly colored by the intangible influence of the subjective responses engendered by the particular other. Conversation cannot be catalogued as merely the cumulative product of separate and unrelated individual efforts, but, on the contrary, it is rather a synthesized whole that is indivisibly welded by the interaction of the parties involved. As a participant in the conversations, the defendant Hotchner would be as much an architect thereof as any of the other participants. In this case, where most of the quoted conversations took place between the defendant author and the subject of the work, such conversations necessarily reflect a duality that defies dissection or divisibility. In light of the interaction which renders conversation indivisible, it is difficult to see how conversation can be held to constitute the sort of individual intellectual production to which protection is afforded by way of a common law copyright.

Moreover, while plaintiff emphasizes the quantitative extent to which her husband's conversational expressions are used in the book and attempts to spell out therefrom a separate literary property, she overlooks a vital factor. These random and disconnected oral conversations are given some semblance of form only by virtue of their arrangement in the context of the defendant author's literary creation. Standing completely alone they are merely a disoriented conglomeration of unconnected expressions. It is the manner of defendant's incorporation and presentation of these conversational segments that organizes them into a coherent format and renders them meaningful. It is clear, therefore, that plaintiff has failed to establish any right to a common law copyright to any portion of the book in question, and her claim in that regard must necessarily be held insufficient to warrant the injunctive relief sought.

The preliminary injunction was denied and the book was thereafter published. Then there was an application for final relief.
On March 21st, 1967 a second court case ESTATE OF ERNEST HEMINGWAY AND MARY HEMINGWAY VS. RANDOM HOUSE AND A.E. HOTCHNER took place at the New York County Supreme Court. In his opinion, Judge Mitchell Schweitzer stated:

Biographies, of course, are fundamentally personal histories and it is both reasonable and customary for biographers to refer to and utilize earlier works dealing with the subject of the work and occasionally to quote directly from such works. [...]

Can Ernest Hemingway or his representatives assert any literary property right in his oral conversations with Hotchner? In denying a temporary injunction in this case, Justice Frank pointed to a number of good reasons for denying any such rights. Conversations, [Frank] said, are inevitably the product of interaction between the parties; they are not individual intellectual productions. Plaintiffs seek to escape the thrust of this argument by alleging that Hemingway's contributions to these conversations were unique and self-sufficient and amounted to literary compositions in themselves. To permit this contention to prevail would immerse this court, and others in future cases, in an impossible inquiry. How can anyone ever measure the relative self-sufficiency of one party's contributions to a dialogue? Volume is no measure, surely, as the few words of one participant may evoke the lengthier expressions of the other. Subjective inquiry into the quality of the expressions of each would be invidious and unproductive. Should we have a rule based on the relative fame or respective professions of the participants? Again, this is not the kind of measurement from which a court could fashion just results. In the instant case, both parties are writers. One is surely more famed than the other, but how can this court presume that that proves anything at all about their conversations with one another? Mr. Hotchner is a successful professional in his own right, and to deny him the use of his conversations with Hemingway on any such basis would require an assumption of omnipotence this court is not prepared to assume. Any attempt to quantify or otherwise analyze or apportion these elements demonstrates both the futility of the endeavor and the unworthiness of the idea. [...]

It can make no difference that, as is admitted, the author here obtained some of his materials from tape recordings he had made. That they were recorded does not change the character of the utterances. It is recognized that under some circumstances, such as where the speaker was in effect dictating to a passive receiver, he might have a claim to property in the recorded material. Too, were the recordings unlawfully made, other considerations would arise. But in the case there is no evidence other than that Hotchner used his recordings as an occasional substitute and supplement for memory or note-taking. In this respect he has done no more than take advantage of a modern technique for preserving for posterity the raw materials of history."

It was concluded, therefore, that the defendants were granted summary judgment dismissing all four causes of action. Then the Estate of Hemingway appealed.

On December 12th, 1968 a third court case ESTATE OF ERNEST HEMINGWAY VS. RANDOM HOUSE took place at the Court of Appeals of New York. In his opinion, Chief Judge Fuld stated:

> The underlying rationale for common law copyright is applicable regardless of whether such labor assumes tangible form. The principle that it is not the tangible embodiment of the author's work but the creation of the work itself which is protected finds recognition in a number of ways in copyright law. One example, with some relevance to the problem before us, is the treatment which the law has accorded to personal letters—a kind of half-conversation in written form. Although the paper upon which the letter is written belongs to the recipient, it is the author who has the right to public them or to prevent their publication. Nor has speech itself been entirely without protection against reproduction for publication. The public delivery of an address or a lecture or the performance of a play is not deemed a 'publication,' and, accordingly, it does not deprive the author of his common law copyright in its contents. Letters, however—like plays and public addresses, written or not—have distinct, identifiable boundaries and they are, in most cases, only occasional products. Whatever difficulties attend the formulation of suitable rules for the enforcement of rights in such works, they are relatively manageable. However, conversational speech, the distinctive behavior of man, is quite another matter, and subjecting any part of it to the restraints of copyright presents unique problems. One such problem—and it was stressed by judge Schweitzer that of avoiding undue restraints on the freedoms of speech and press and, in particular, on the writers of history and of biographical works safeguarding of essential freedoms in this area—is, though, not without its complications. The indispensable right of the press to report on what people have done, or on what has happened to them or on what they have said in public does not necessarily imply an unbounded freedom to publish whatever they may have said in private conversation, any more than it implies a freedom to copy and publish what people may have put down in private writings. [...]
>
> Copyright, both common law and statutory, rests on the assumption that there are forms of expression, limited in kind, to be sure, which should not be divulged to the public without the consent of their author. The purpose, far from being restrictive, is to encourage and protect intellectual labor. [...]

> Assuming, without deciding, that in a proper case a common law copyright in certain limited kinds of spoken dialogue might be recognized, it would, at the very least, be required that the speaker indicate that he intended to mark off the utterance in question from the ordinary stream of speech, that he meant to adopt it as a unique statement and that he wished to exercise control over its publication. In the conventional common law copyright situation, this indication is afforded by the creation of the manuscript itself. It would have to be evidenced in some other way if protection were ever to be accorded to some forms of conversational dialogue. Another way of formulating such a rule might be to say that, although, in the case of most intellectual products, the courts are reluctant to find that an author has 'published,' so as to lose his common law copyright, in the case of conversational speech—because of its unique nature—there should be a presumption that the speaker has not reserved any common law rights unless the contrary strongly appears. However, we need not carry such speculation further in the present case since the requisite conditions are plainly absent here. [...]

> For present purposes, it is enough to observe that Hemingway's words and conduct, far from making any such reservation, left no doubt of his willingness to permit Hotchner to draw freely on their conversation in writing about him and to publish such material. What we have said disposes of the plaintiffs' claim both to exclusive and to joint copyright and we need not consider this aspect of the case any further. It follows, therefore, that the courts below were eminently correct in dismissing the first cause of action.

In their conclusion the courts dismissed the complaint and affirmed the orders appealed. The result is that CONVERSATIONS CAN BE COPYRIGHTED, BUT ONLY IF ONE OF THE SPEAKERS INDICATES BY WORDS OR CIRCUMSTANCES THAT HE OR SHE INTENDS TO MARK OFF HER UTTERANCES. ∎

HERE TODAY – GONE TOMORROW!

THE

REGURGITATING
LADY

WHOSE EMETIC POWER

HAS EXCITED THE IMAGINATION OF ALL THOSE WHO HAVE
LOVED & LOST, At Long Last Returns –

A GOLD WISHBONE
A PORCELAIN FIGURINE
A DOG CALLED MAGGIE

BEHOLD Engraved Heirlooms Returned To Once-Careless Daughters; SEE
Abandoned Treasures Handed Back To Grown Men; WATCH Lost Letters Delivered, Snatched Handbags Recovered, Family Fortunes Restored.

!! A DIVINE ACT OF FATE AND POSSESSION !!
! A SELFLESS GESTURE OF CHARITY !

WELCOME BACK WITH A GASP

Things STOLEN, Things MISPLACED, Things FORGOTTEN

COME ONE — COME ALL

THE MUNDANE AND THE VALUABLE; THE ADORED AND DISCARDED.

coins, shoes, glasses, keys; hats, umbrellas, diaries, et cetera.

FINAL DAY.

THE SAME LOCATION, FRIDAY NOVEMBER 31, 7PM.

INT. REORIENTED TO THE EAST. TONIGHT THE 2 LECTERNS ARE ACCOMPANIED
BY AN EMPTY WOODEN EASEL TO THE LEFT AND AN OVERHEAD PROJECTOR AT
CENTRE. IT IS HALLOWEEN, PUNCTUATED BY THE NOTES OF AN ENDLESSLY RISING
CANON (ALSO KNOWN AS THE 'SHEPHERD'S TONE').

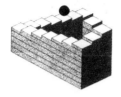 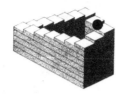 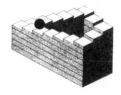

etc.

D AND S ENTER THROUGH AN ARCH ON THE LEFT AND OCCUPY THEIR REGULAR
LECTERNS. THE RISING CANON ENDS ABRUPTLY. SILENCE. THEY PROCEED TO
DELIVER, WORD FOR WORD, THE SAME INTRODUCTION AS THE PREVIOUS EVENINGS.
THEN S CONTINUES.

S: In tonight's first piece David is going to explain some elementary mathematics, and he'll use an overhead projector to walk you step by step through the idea. Now, although I know the title—not least because we've previously published a different piece under the same name—I'm not sure exactly where to place the emphasis; I'm not sure whether I should read it as NAÏVE SET THEORY, NAÏVE SET THEORY, or NAÏVE SET THEORY. In the end, I suspect it's all three at once, and I further suspect this is precisely the point of the talk. David ...

D PICKS UP THE RIGHT LECTERN AND MOVES IT ADJACENT TO THE OVERHEAD
PROJECTOR, PRECARIOUSLY BALANCED ON AN UPENDED WOODEN SHELF IN
FRONT OF THE AUDIENCE. TRANSPARENCIES ARE SHUFFLED, THOUGHTS
COLLECTED. THE FIRST ACETATE IS LAID DOWN ON PROJECTOR BED. D BEGINS
TO READ FROM IT.

SOME years ago, being with a camping party in the mountains, I returned from a solitary ramble to find every one engaged in a ferocious metaphysical dispute. The *corpus* of the dispute was a squirrel — a live squirrel supposed to be clinging to one side of a tree-trunk; while over against the tree's opposite side a human being was imagined to stand. This human witness tries to get sight of the squirrel by moving rapidly round the tree, but no matter how fast he goes, the squirrel moves as fast in the opposite direction, and always keeps the tree between himself and the man, so that never a glimpse of him is caught. The resultant metaphysical problem now is this: *Does the man go round the squirrel or not?*

D CONTINUES.

He goes round the tree, sure enough, and the squirrel is on the tree; but does he go round the squirrel? In the unlimited leisure of the wilderness, discussion had been worn threadbare. Everyone had taken sides, and was obstinate; and the numbers on both sides were even. Each side, when I appeared therefore appealed to me to make it a majority. Mindful of the scholastic adage that whenever you meet a contradiction you must make a distinction, I immediately sought and found one, as follows: "Which party is right," I said, "depends on what you *practically mean* by 'going round' the squirrel. If you mean passing from the north of him to the east, then to the south, then to the west, and then to the north of him again, obviously the man does go round him, for he occupies these successive positions. But if on the contrary you mean being first in front of him, then on the right of him, then behind him, then on his left, and finally in front again, it is quite as obvious that the man fails to go round him, for by the compensating movements the squirrel makes, he keeps his belly turned towards the man all the time, and his back turned away. Make the distinction, and there is no occasion for any farther dispute. You are both right and both wrong according as you conceive the verb 'to go round' in one practical fashion or the other."

William James

Pragmatism

The excerpt that I just read comes from this book   , which is relevant here for a couple of reasons. First—the book is the printed translation of a series of spoken lectures that William James gave at Harvard University in 1907. It's unclear whether the texts published in this book are transcriptions of his speech or scripts for his speeches. Most likely it's some synthesis of the two. The second reason this book is important tonight is for its subtitle—PRAGMATISM, A NEW NAME FOR SOME OLD WAYS OF THINKING—which I think is quite nice. Why this title is directly relevant should become clear over the course of the talk.

The book was given to me by Anthony Huberman, a curator and friend in New York, as part of a group reading project that he and Larissa Harris initiated for their ongoing exhibition series, 'The Steins'. For one such 'exhibition', this volume was passed around a number of readers, all of whom left their notes in the margins. I'll be showing some of these noted pages. My talk is organized around three books—this one is the first—with some notes, diagrams and equations in between. Although the talk will be at least substantively about mathematics and logic, I hope it is at least equally about something else at the same time.

William James   was a professor at Harvard University where he helped to define and develop the discipline of psychology.

92

He was trained as a medical doctor. He was widely read. He was born into a substantial New England family, the son of Henry James, Sr. and the brother of the novelist Henry James, Jr. His studies and free-ranging mind led him from psychology into logic, theology and mathematics. He might even be called America's first philosopher, if that's not a contradiction. (As an American, I'm allowed to say that.)

In PRAGMATISM, James makes an important distinction between two classes of thinking central to his argument and offers terms for each. He names the pair of terms 'rationalist' and 'empiricist,' 'empiricist' meaning your lover of facts in all their crude variety, 'rationalist' meaning your devotee to abstract and eternal principles. No one can live an hour without both facts and principles, so it is a difference rather of emphasis. The RATIONALIST sees the world as Eternal, Fixed, Complete, Total and Absolute. By contrast, the EMPIRICIST believes that the world is Temporary, Changing, Incomplete, Partial and Contingent. William James' PRAGMATISM wholeheartedly embraces the EMPIRICIST view. Following from the idea that the world is unfinished, James borrowed the name PRAGMATISM from another philosopher (a close friend, 30 years his senior) because he believed that the idea was incomplete.

PRAGMATISM was originally described by the mathematician Charles Sanders Pierce in his article 'How to Make Our Ideas Clear,' in the 'Popular Science Monthly' for January of that year[1] Mr. Peirce, after pointing out that our beliefs are really rules for action, said that, to develop a thought's meaning, we need only determine what conduct it is fitted to produce: that conduct is for us its sole significance. And the tangible fact at the root of all our thought-distinctions, however subtle, is that there is no one of them so fine as to consist in anything but a possible difference of practice. To attain perfect clearness in our thoughts of an object, then, we need only consider what conceivable effects of a practical kind the object may involve — what sensations we are to expect from it, and what reactions we must prepare. Our conception of these effects, whether immediate or remote, is then for us the whole of our conception of the object, so far as that conception has positive significance at all. Pierce named this method of producing truth PRAGMATISM and he equated it directly with EMPIRICISM. William James took Pierce's PRAGMATISM plus David Hume's EMPIRICISM to describe a RADICAL EMPIRICISM that forms the basis of his PRAGMATIC METHOD. He describes it crisply here where I've marked an asterisk

No particular results then, so far, but only an attitude of orientation, is what the pragmatic method means. *The attitude of looking away from first things, principles, 'categories,' supposed necessities; and of looking towards last things, fruits, consequences, facts.*

A SMALL BREATH. HE CONTINUES.

The PRAGMATIC METHOD then actually PRODUCES TRUTH by considering what practical consequences in the world a particular condition being either true or false will have. It is ONLY based on these effects that a given condition is said to be either true or not. (James describes this calculus as the practical cash-value of an idea.) This method for uncovering truth necessarily progresses OVER TIME and, crucially, ONLY IN ONE DIRECTION as a process that unfolds irrevocably FORWARD. James quotes Søren Kierkegaard saying:

We live forwards, a Danish thinker has said, but we understand backwards.*

*[James is referring to Sören Kierkegaard (1813–1855).]

Please take special note of this—as we're going to come back to it later.

Now, if I were to try to translate this distinction between RATIONALIST and PRAGMATIST into another system as a simple

graphic diagram, I might reasonably use this circle ⭕ to stand for the RATIONALIST. The RATIONALIST insists that the world is one sealed, perfect and knowable system. Truths are eternal and absolute—they need only to be discovered through reasoned and logical investigation. Meanwhile, for the PRAGMATIST the world looks more

like this ⭕.

D DRAWS CIRCLE CONTINUOUSLY, IMPERFECTLY, ON THE O-H-P WHILE CONTINUING.

The PRAGMATIST insists that the world is always becoming and that truth CAN ONLY BE PRODUCED THROUGH PRACTICE. For the PRAGMATIST, time is an arrow that marches forward and truth comes along for the ride.

A BRIEF SHUFFLING OF ACETATES WHILE REACHING BELOW TO PICK UP THE SECOND BOOK.

The next book I'd like to talk about is **Kurt Gödel ON FORMALLY UNDECIDABLE PROPOSITIONS OF PRINCIPIA MATHEMATICA AND RELATED SYSTEMS**. Written in 1931 by Austrian mathematician Kurt Gödel, this book has been said to contain the largest idea of the 20th century. Gödel spent the majority of his academic career at the Institute for Advanced Studies at Princeton University, a free-thinking playground for fellows paid to produce original research with no particular publishing or teaching responsibilities. Albert Einstein, a fellow fellow at the Institute famously said the best thing about being there was the walk home each day with

Kurt . Now, I'm going to try roughly explain the idea

94

which is at the center of Gödel's paper to you. We will be passing through some advanced mathematics and I can assure you that I understand it just well enough to get through this talk here this evening. But first, it is important to have a little background on the state of mathematics (and METAMATHEMATICS.) leading up to 1931 and Kurt Gödel's paper

ON FORMALLY UNDECIDABLE
PROPOSITIONS
OF PRINCIPIA MATHEMATICA
AND RELATED SYSTEMS . The British mathematician-philosophers Bertrand Russell and Alfred North Whitehead published PRINCIPIA MATHEMATICA (1910–13) and exhibited the fundamental parts of mathematics, including arithmetic, as a *deductive system* starting from a limited number of axioms, in which each theorem is shown to follow logically from the axioms and theorems which precede it according to a limited number of rules of inference. The PRINCIPIA MATHEMATICA attempted to capture all of mathematics in one complete, total and RATIONAL system. In this classically epic project (and its correspondingly large volume) Russell and Whitehead were convinced that they had reconciled all branches of mathematics into one coherent and total AXIOMATIC framework. AXIOMATIC is a term used to describe a mathematic system that proceeds from first overall rules through deductive reasoning, to account for all possible results. So, this system begins with a set of first rules or AXIOMS from which THEOREMS are derived and used to account for all possible STATEMENTS. The entire AXIOMATIC system is calculated, top-down, through a chain of logical deductive reasoning and a sequence of formulas (also known as a CALCULUS.)

But this correspondence between calculus and deductive system may be viewed in reverse, instead of marching from AXIOM to THEOREM to STATEMENT through a series of equations, you can proceed from STATEMENT to THEOREM to AXIOM through IN-ductive, rather than DE-ductive calculations. You begin at the simplest mathematical STATEMENT (for example, 1 + 1 = 2 (which is also nicely called a mathematical SENTENCE)) and proceed step-by-step to greater and greater abstraction (STATEMENT >> THEOREM >> AXIOM) ARRIVING AT FIRST RULES, LAST.

As opposed to a deductive, logical and complete AXIOMATIC approach, this inductive, from zero and incomplete method might reasonably be called NAÏVE. (We'll use this term anyway—as often in mathematics, a generically descriptive word is given a precise meaning.)

Then, the simplest way for me to explain the distinction between an AXIOMATIC and NAÏVE approach is by talking about how each would attempt to describe the set of whole numbers (in other words, all of the whole positive integers). In an AXIOMATIC system, the set of whole numbers would be defined as

WHOLE NUMBERS = { 0, 1, 2, 3 ... }

In this way, the whole set of whole numbers is assumed to contain infinitely many members. By contrast, a NAÏVE approach to the same definition of the set of WHOLE NUMBERS would mean Starting with 0, 1 is defined as the immediate successor of 0, 2 as the immediate successor of 1, and so on.

The NAÏVE approach does not assume that the set contains an infinity of members, but rather that it simply contains all of the members (numbers) that have (so far) been counted. In another minute, the set will contain more numbers, and so on and so on and so on. The AXIOMATIC approach assumes instead that the set arrives all at once, COMPLETE, with infinitely many members—all of the WHOLE NUMBERS—infinity in the palm of your hand. Perhaps this distinction between AXIOMATIC and NAÏVE may remind you of the previous difference between RATIONAL and PRAGMATIC a little while back.

NOW, Kurt Gödel had an intuition that the complete and rational system that Russell and Whitehead had laid out in PRINCIPIA MATHEMATICA was not nearly as rational or as complete as they claimed. And he was pretty sure that he could prove that even the simplest of all mathematics—plain whole number arithmetic ($1 + 1 = 2$)—was INCOMPLETE and relied on at least assumption from outside of its own mathematical system. In order to PROVE (rigorously and mathematically) this idea within mathematics, Gödel could use only mathematic reasoning. However, mathematical statements have a funny quality—that is, any statement about mathematics is only a statement OF mathematics and never a statement ABOUT mathematics. For example, a mathematical sentence such as

$$1 + 1 = 2$$

means only what it says and can only use this limited (well, actually, infinitely limited) alphabet of the set of whole numbers to express itself. However, Gödel found his way out of this bind by DEVISING A SECOND SET OF NUMBERS. What he does is to provide a co-ordinating rule according to which a different number (which I shall call a *Gödel number*) is assigned to each string in his formal system. The rule also works in reverse: of every number 0, 1, 2, 3, etc. the rule determines whether the number is the Gödel number of a basic sign, or of a series of basic signs, or of a series of series of basic signs, so, together with the set of whole numbers

$$\{ 0, 1, 2, 3 \dots \}$$

which can be used to form the sentence

$$1 + 1 = 2$$

Gödel introduced the second set of numbers, the Gödel Numbers (which I'll write from here on with "quotes") refer instead to an entire mathematical sentence so

$$"3" = (1 + 1 = 2).$$

And, following from that, then you could say

$$"3" + "3" = (1 + 1 = 2) + (1 + 1 = 2)$$

and so on and so on. Gödel used his second set of meta-numbers to

CHAPTER 8

AN OLD FRIEND

Unable to see beyond the trees, and my attention diverted to the task of processing Dick's information about our whereabouts, I hadn't yet noticed that the banks of the ribbon of water, that I had recognised from the top, had shifted to meet us here at the end of the avenue. The hill we had walked down earlier, now to our left, was in effect the steep bank of the wide river to our right, whose opposite bank was no longer perfectly canal-parallel to the one we stood on, but was quite a way off towards the sea. The banks were no longer the concrete sidings that I used to dangle my legs off as I threw stones in to pass the time, but smooth, tree-lined and root-ridden tracks that ran down into the water.

Where the trees stopped, the river cut further inwards and a path ran along its length, from here out towards what I imagined to be Seabrook. We stopped at a long building, whose facade comprised of three successive two-storey arches built of red brick and framed with darker brown ones. Each arch was topped by an equilateral triangle of the same arrangement of bricks, with a vent in each, from which came a trickle of smoke. The side of the building, extending back towards the hill, was built of much larger, rougher grey stones, in which windows and a large red-painted metal door were set, where all who came in or out were forced to duck. The arches at the front, however, allowed for the tallest guest to enter and sit at the long tables in the three halls inside, or on the balconies overlooking them, and look out over the water while enjoying a drink or the company of others.

Dick started to walk again, and we left the building behind and continued along the banks of the river. As we talked, a steady white presence filled my peripheral vision, never leaving or entering my sight until I turned to look at it directly: the wind was so still that five boats kept pace, as though they were walking with us. Looking over, I read the first texts I had seen since leaving home that morning:

The ROSIE

The WELCOME

The Flying Foam

The GLEANER

An Old Friend

Some of the fores were hand-painted in italics that sloped in the opposite direction of the course of the stern. Others were, port and starboard, perpendicular to the plimsoll line. Dick told me—as though foreseeing my inevitable question—that it was customary for boats to be permanently marked with their given names, it being bad luck for them to be re-named. This only held in the case of boats, he added.

He told me how children played a game: They would write the word "apple" on an apple (for example), and give it to someone else. The person who received and read this labelled object would experience something that he now faintly experienced with these boats: Common Knowledge would be short-circuited and withheld by the label, and a slight mental resonance would occur in the mind of the beholder, described by most as somehow similar to pins and needles, or a dead-leg. The boats are the only cases where it is impossible to gain further knowledge, because their names hold no relation to their specific properties.

Surely the markings *were* part of the same specific properties, I noted.

For a while, Dick continued in silence. Then he stopped and sat down by a small inlet that flowed in from the river into a garden besides by the bank. But my curiosity had got the better of our conversation, and I then asked how it was possible to point things out to each other in everyday speech? Dick looked at me with the same expression as when we had first met, and told me it was simply not necessary, but he admitted that he had never (", ever") heard this kind of information come out of his, nor anyone's mouth until today. It had been a strange experience for him to 'speak' and share Common Knowledge with me. He had never known what it could be like to tell something that everyone already knew.

Go on, I said.

But he sat in silence, clearly struggling to rationalise what he was going through, staring at the water level rising and falling in the inlet. We watched, as four stepping stones to the other side were slowly being covered as the micro-tide flowed in, held its height for about twenty seconds, then fell. The stones were exposed again, and tiny whirlpools formed around their streamlined edges, visualised by the stray cress-like weeds that grew, rootless, in the water. As the water was pulled out towards the sea, the leaves span clockwise on the sea side edges of the stones. It came back in, and they washed round the edges to gather—on the far side— and turn the opposite way.

Standing and seeing Dick staring, I held out my hand, grabbed his and pulled him up. We crossed the stepping stones, and walked up the stream into the gardens on the other side. A startled group of black-birds, foraging on the lawns, sounded the alarm with what sounded like a penny whis-tle that had been attached to a motorbike exhaust-pipe, and flew off into the nearby bushes, accompanied by a larger feathered flash of bright green and yellow, asking to be followed. Dick, shook out of his meditation, started to explain what it felt like for him to name names. Striding off ahead, for me to

follow along the shingle paths that allowed
us to pass through the dense growths of various types of flowers that weren't planted
but just grew there together; his arms shot
out in all directions, randomly picking out
certain flowers, pointing and reeling off:

"[So there's]   GOLDEN SUNSHINE
[and]   PLEASANT JOURNEY   ,
                 GEISHA GOWN
[and there's]   TOTENKO
[and there's]   GEISHA HISKIKI   .

[There's]   LASTING PLEASURE   !
[and there's]   ENCHANTED MELODY
[there's]   WALLA BEAUTY   .
[There's]   ELECTRIC RAYS
[and there's]   PIN STRIPE

[There's]   BLACK SWAN   .
[There's]   MOLTEN EMBERS   !
[And that's]   NATIVE CHIEF
[that's]   NEW SNOW   ,
[and that's]   REAL DELIGHT   .

103

An Old Friend

[That's]	GAYLIGHT	,
[]	MUSIC-HALL	,
[]	PROSPERITY	,
[]	VIOLET HARMONY	
[and]	ARTIC FANCY	
[And there's]	SECOND LOOK	!
[And that's]	SOCIALITE	.
[And that's]	AUTUMN LEAVES	
[and that's]	TEAL WOOD	
[and that's]	MOUNTAIN LAKE	!
[There's]	SORCEROR'S LAKE	,
[there's]	TIME AND TIDE	.
[There's]	GUSTO	,
[there's]	POPULAR DEMAND	
[and that's]	GOOD SHOW."	

From the past hours' exchanges and conversations, Dick was well aware of my strangeness to his surroundings. Yet I think that my presence was starting to have a similar effect of wonder about his own observations of his surroundings, as his did on mine. My specific questions about the differences in the place

I thought I knew were answered so well, that he wasn't merely "showing me around", as he had put it. He began to understand that I was not merely a tourist needing to know the ins-and-outs, but someone who was in turn, showing him what it was he took for granted. I was grateful of his company, and until now, the factual nature of a lot of his answers seemed like he had learned everything he told me by heart, or was being prompted by lines that were given to him to recite. I thought of another question in order to better understand this situation, or perhaps even get out of it: I asked him what had happened to the canal, and why it was so much wider.

He caught his breath, and (pointing back in the direction of his words) began a short account of how, by 2084, the sea level had risen high enough to pass over the lock at the Seabrook end and become The Canal River estuary, submerging the original banking as it ran in, filling up Imperial Lake. It took forty years for the erosion to stabilise, the re-structuring of the surrounding land

105

being merely a cause of the lunar tides. The inhabitants of the Romney, Hythe and Dymchurch Islands relocated between 2075 and 83, and in 2100, it was made known that people could set up shop there again. However, most people had already found their neighbours after The Transportation Notice, and felt little need to break the ties that they had worked so long and hard for. So the islands became public oyster flats.

"Mmmmm."

I tried to picture a series of mental satellite images over a timeline, based on what he was telling me. But, once again, my attention became absorbed by my immediate surroundings. By the time we had reached Seabrook, the tide was starting to go out, and the river's level slowly dropped to expose long stretches of black rocks running along its banks, into the estuary and along the green seacoast. The boats had steered away from the banks towards deeper waters, out into the Channel. Dick took me up a wooded hill to a cliff top, and from up there we watched as two young couples entered through the woods and walked over the sandy river bed, onto the rocks, and slowly began picking their way across, sideways, taking the next step forward as and when the tide allowed. From above, we could just make out the short exchanges between them. All four were bent over, gazing down at the rocks; picking, inspecting, and filling large bags as they moved. Every day, Dick said, the rocks replenished themselves enough to give these people, their needs and weather permitting, a daily supply of mussels and oysters ("during the months with an 'r' in them"), and allowed them in turn to feed at least six others when they got home.

The shadows grew longer, and the colourful-yet-muted clothing of the four gradually became black when backlit by the setting sun. They seemed to sense that it was time to get back, and gathered their way, step by step. They poured their collected harvest into one bag, of which the two men took a handle each, and headed over the beds, and up the banks towards us.

An Old Friend

"Cmon." said Dick, and started off down hill, to the sea shore, walking to the East towards Sandgate. We joined the growing number of people who were heading places before the evening set in, and strolled along the esplanade. People looked at me as we passed, and their short greetings and exchanges were mingled with the constant sound of shingle being swept smooth to our right. The first of many wooden-sided, two-storey houses, raised a few metres above the beach, appeared before us as we walked into the village. Again, we passed through what seemed to be one large back garden belonging to all of these houses, where vegetables were tended, and tables stood where people sat working and exchanging words.

As the sun went down we took a turn back towards the sea and to the foot of a small hill, upon which grew tall pine trees at an angle. I still had a burning question that had gone unexplained from before:

"What's the transportation notice?"

"I won't say 'It's funny you should ask.'

but I'm taking you to someone who will put us up for the night. He won't let you sleep though, once he understands all you need to know. He's one of our oldest neighbours, and has much more to tell you, from experience, than I ever could. I thought I would bring you to him since he knows more of all that has happened within the last two hundred years than anybody else does.

"We'll be at the house in a minute. He's getting too old to do much work anymore. He was custodian of the books for many years; but he still lives amongst them. He looks upon himself as a part of the books, or the books a part of him, I don't know which. Years ago, people started donating their books to him, as he seemed like the only person who would still find a use for them. One by one, the other people in the house moved out, to make room for what slowly grew into what he still calls 'the library'. Many people stop by to visit him with a question, but not many people actually end up consulting the books. He'll tell you anything you want to know.

An Old Friend

"But listen to me rambling on when you're just about to meet him anyway. Sorry. You asked me about the Transportation Notice. This is it:" (Dick paused and began reciting again, only this time his voice took on a slightly different tone than before)

"ON THIS DAY,
SEPTEMBER FIFTEENTH,
TWO-THOUSAND AND
TWENTY-THREE,
AN AGREEMENT HAS BEEN MADE
FOR THE PUBLICK GOOD:
FOR REASONS THAT ARE
COMMON KNOWLEDGE,
MOTORISED TRANSPORTATION
OF PEOPLE OR GOODS
WILL NEVER TAKE PLACE,
AGAIN, FROM NEW YEAR'S DAY,
TWENTY-TWENTY-NINE, ONWARDS!

IT HAS BEEN DEDUCED
THAT MOTORISED TRANSPORTA-
TION OF PEOPLE OR GOODS
IS NOT NECESSARY.

110

EVERY PERSON HAS FIVE YEARS
TO STATE WHERE THEY WISH TO LIVE,
WHO THEY PROPOSE
TO BE THEIR NEIGHBOURS AND
HOW THEY WISH TO CO-OPERATE.
DETAILED ADVICE ON RELOCATION
AND ALTERNATIVE, CO-OPERATIVE
PRODUCTION FORMS WILL BECOME
COMMON KNOWLEDGE.
MAKE YOUR INITIAL PLANS KNOWN
A.S.A.P:
IDEAL SITUATIONS WILL ONLY
BE FOUND AFTER SEVERAL YEARS
OF COLLECTIVE CALCULATION."

"Here we are."

He stopped in front of a large white building
in the middle of a sloping, terraced garden
that ran all the way down to the beach. We
stood on the path at the 'front', signalled by
the large blue double door, which looked
like it hadn't been used for a long time. To
the right a set of stairs ran up to smaller door
on the first floor. To the left, a thick white

111

An Old Friend

concrete frame around a blue painted gate with the words "GARDEN FLAT" on it.

Dick opened the gate and walked in. I followed as he took me down a set of uneven brown stone stairs, into the garden, then back up again, up another set that wound anti-clockwise around an inset corner of the building. Jutting and looking out over the sea, was a wood-framed glass sun-room with a sloping, grey tiled roof, on stilts above gardens similar to those we had just passed through, yet this one was possibly even more exuberant and wild. Dick knocked, and as we stood at the door, I took in the complete one-hundred-and-eighty degree view of the sea, over the line of the Channel to the symmetrical French cliffs on the other side. The only thing that broke this panorama was a large American oak, with a deeply engrained grey bark that had been blasted by the salt and sea winds, and the largest fig tree I had ever seen on these shores, growing next to it.

create a self-referential mathematical statement. And although I'll admit that I only partially understand what this means, I can intuitively understand why it has been called the biggest idea of the 20th century. By using mathematics to talk about itself, Gödel was able to use the same mathematical logic to PROVE, rigorously and WITHIN ITS OWN SYSTEM, that all mathematical logic is INCOMPLETE. All mathematics, even simple arithmetic, ALWAYS RELIES ON AT LEAST ONE ASSUMPTION THAT CANNOT BE PROVED WITHIN ITS OWN SYSTEM. Gödel found at the centre of mathematics—that temple of rational thought and logical abstract reasoning—a gaping hole. MATHEMATIC TRUTH WAS ABSOLUTELY NOT ABSOLUTE.

Gödel's self-referential mathematic statement is easier to understand translated into English. So the sentence

This statement is false.

has a similar logic. As soon as you agree that "This sentence is false" is true, then it cancels itself. Try it yourself—it sets off a repeating loop with no obvious exit. It is a self-referential, but also self-contradicting, statement. Even extending this statement over two sentences as in

The following statement is true.
The previous statement is false.

only lengthens the loop. But, Gödel's mathematical sentence translated into English could be

This statement is neither true nor false.

which is of course neither true nor false. By creating a pretzel logic that is both itself and truly about itself, Gödel found a way out of this infinite loop and in the process he described another way of understanding the world, the whole world, as absolutely, radically incomplete. Mathematical truth MUST ALWAYS BE PRODUCED (through practice) and NEVER SIMPLY DISCOVERED.

Translating Gödel's idea into a third system as a simple graphic figure, one might begin with a simple triangle which, with a few more lines added here and there becomes the Penrose or Impossible Triangle which Stuart mentioned in his introduction as some kind of possible mascot for this set of talks, this issue. The impossible triangle also appears in the photogram by Walead Beshty that's hanging on the wall behind me [gestures over left shoulder] and is on the cover of the issue. If you begin to follow this quasi-three-dimensional figure from any corner proceeding around its surface, the surface appears continuous and correct. However, if you consider the entire figure, you may quickly conclude that it is an impossible shape! The Penrose Triangle has been called "impossibility in its purest form."

At every moment along its tracing, the figure is possible, but as soon as you attempt to reconcile the entire shape, you realize that it's not possible. Kurt Gödel would say simply, it is INCOMPLETE.

AGAIN REACHING DOWN BELOW THE BASE OF THE OVERHEAD PROJECTOR, D PULLS OUT THE THIRD BOOK AND HOLDS IT UP FOR THE AUDIENCE.

The final book that I'd like to talk about tonight is   . Completed in 1960, Paul R. Halmos' NAÏVE SET THEORY is an introductory textbook for aspiring mathematicians to the complexities of

Set Theory. Paul Halmos   was a Hungarian mathematician who spent the largest part of his academic career in southern California at UC-Santa Barbara. A distinguished mathematician in his own right, Halmos is best known for series of three pop-mathematic books called HOW TO WRITE MATHEMATICS, HOW TO READ MATHEMATICS and HOW TO SPEAK MATHEMATICS. As an exemplary explainer of abstract logic, Halmos was at least equally interested in how to communicate this abstract body of knowledge in a manner equal to its inherent beauty.

Paul Halmos is also immortalized as a typographical sign. This is a mathematic proof of the statement $1 + 1 = 2$:

$*54 \cdot 43$. $\vdash : . \alpha, \beta \in 1 . \supset : \alpha \cap \beta = \Lambda . \equiv . \alpha \cup \beta \in 2$

  Dem.

  $\vdash . *54 \cdot 26 . \supset \vdash : . \alpha = \iota'x . \beta = \iota'y . \supset : \alpha \cup \beta \in 2 . \equiv . x \neq y .$
  $[*51 \cdot 231] \qquad\qquad\qquad\qquad\qquad\qquad \equiv . \iota'x \cap \iota'y = \Lambda .$
  $[*13 \cdot 12] \qquad\qquad\qquad\qquad\qquad\qquad \equiv . \alpha \cap \beta = \Lambda \qquad (1)$
  $\vdash . (1) . *11 \cdot 11 \cdot 35 . \supset$
    $\vdash : . (\exists x, y) . \alpha = \iota'x . \beta = \iota'y . \supset : \alpha \cup \beta \in 2 . \equiv . \alpha \cap \beta = \Lambda \qquad (2)$
  $\vdash . (2) . *11 \cdot 54 . *52 \cdot 1 . \supset \vdash . \text{Prop}$

  From this proposition it will follow, when arithmetical addition has been defined, that $1 + 1 = 2$.   ∎

The mark at the end of this proof (after the sequence of largely unintelligible symbolic manipulations which proceed the final result) is a solid black rectangular box (∎) set flush right. This mark (it can also appear in various sizes, filled or unfilled) typically follows the final statement of a proof and replaces the conventional Q.E.D. (or QUAD ERAT DEMONSTRANDUM in Latin, which simply translated means THAT WHICH HAS BEEN DEMONSTRATED.) Halmos began replacing the Latin with this simple box and the typographical symbol now has his name—it is called the 'Halmos'.

114

Halmos begins his PREFACE with a curiously formed sentence:

Every mathematician agrees that every mathematician must know some set theory; the disagreement begins in trying to decide how much is some.

Now, in this simple sentence, Halmos has placed a paradox, or at least a productively complicated idea, that we will return to: if every mathematician agrees that every mathematician must know, then every mathematician agrees (ALSO and AT THE SAME TIME) that he/she must know some Set Theory. This idea of self-reference and self-inclusion is at the center of the mathematics of NAÏVE SET THEORY, which I will try to describe now.

Set Theory is the study of individual things (numbers, ideas, objects) and how these are collected into sets of things, sets of sets of things, sets of sets of sets of things and so forth. Halmos begins by laying out a few fundamental ideas necessary for working with sets. He begins with EXTENSION, which determines how additional members may be included within any particular set. He describes

If A and B are sets and if every element of A is an element of B, we say that A is a *subset* of B, or B *includes* A, and we write

or

$$A \subset B$$
$$B \supset A.$$

(You'll notice the additional symbols that this introduces here.) Halmos continues to describe SPECIFICATION, or how any item is said to be belonging to a set. So,

Let A be the set of all men. The sentence "x is married" is true for some of the elements x of A and false for others

and it can be written

$$\{x \in A : x \text{ is married}\}.$$

A LARGER BREATH. D ASKS THE AUDIENCE IF THEY ARE FOLLOWING ALL OF THIS. AFTER GENERAL DUBIOUS AFFIRMATION HE CONTINUES.

Okay, so Set Theoretical notation is again added here. These simple principles can be followed to their logical end, to build towers of Set Theoretical logic and corresponding symbology, such as

$$A \cap \emptyset = \emptyset,$$
$$A \cap B = B \cap A,$$
$$A \cap (B \cap C) = (A \cap B) \cap C,$$
$$A \cap A = A,$$
$$A \subset B \text{ if and only if } A \cap B = A.$$

It is important, however, that this logic is ALWAYS built incrementally, from simple assertions to more complex arrangements. This NAÏVE approach to Set Theory is in contrast to the AXIOMATIC Set Theory which proceeds from defining rules in a top-down fashion to generate consequent results. A NAÏVE Set Theory assumes always an incomplete accounting of all sets and therefore works its way out of the logical twister that stymied Bertrand Russell: GIVEN a set whose members are defined as all those members that are not members of that set, THEN is that set a member of itself? The NAÏVE SET THEORY that Halmos describes in this book finds a way out by acknowledging, even embracing, the idea that THE SET OF ALL SETS IS ALWAYS, ITSELF, INCOMPLETE.

115

Halmos then gracefully ends his preface with a suggestion which follows logically from his previous arguments: In other words, general set theory is pretty trivial stuff really, but, if you want to be a mathematician, you need some, and here it is; read it, absorb it, and forget it.

P. R. H.

Maybe a less abstract way to understand what Halmos is saying would be through analogy. So, let's take grapes: ONE GRAPE can be reasonably thought of as a MEMBER. And, it belongs to the SET,

A BUNCH OF GRAPES  which, is itself a member of the SET,

A BUNCH OF A BUNCH OF GRAPES and so on and so on.

At Gavin Brown's Enterprise, a gallery in Greenwich Village in New York, I've admired for a while the painted statement that wraps round the façade of the corner building. It says

the whole world + the work = the whole world

It is Work Number 300 by Martin Creed and implies a worldview in the form of a simple mathematical equation that seems to embed the logic of NAÏVE SET THEORY. Underlying this simple sentence is again simple Set Theory. The set of the WHOLE WORLD contains everything in the whole world and the WORK is a thing in the WHOLE WORLD, so then the WHOLE WORLD must necessarily completely contain the WORK. Adding the WORK back to the WHOLE WORLD leaves you again with only the WHOLE WORLD. This idea of art-making echoes the ideas of James, Gödel and Halmos. The WORK is PRODUCED ONLY BY PRACTICE and IS ONLY ADDED to the WHOLE WORLD which, although it contains every thing in the WHOLE WORLD, is also, by definition, incomplete. VERY lovely.

This is a photograph by Jason Fulford which Stuart commissioned about a year ago or so. It's an album cover from an obscure German popstar Ulrich Roski, made sometime in the 1970s.

And this is a photograph Jason sent me a

few weeks ago that he made while cleaning out his files. I'm not sure if you can see this clearly, but on top of the original album cover is the Polaroid proof that Jason made for that final image. I suppose, or I hope anyway, that it is clear at this point in my talk why this might be interesting. Certainly, the recursive containers of Ulrich Roskis are interesting enough, but what is even more compelling to me is the way that this photograph immediately reveals a specific process of it's own construction that can ONLY HAPPEN FORWARD IN TIME—the original image, then the collaged cover image, then the Polaroid proof and finally this collapsed composite photograph. Time moves in one direction and this final result is ONLY PRODUCED BY PRACTICE.

Now, to translate Halmos' logic into a simple, graphic form we could

draw this rectangle ▭ . Remember this is also the typographical mark, the 'Halmos', used to mark the end of a proof. However, as Gödel (and William James) proved conclusively, every proof ALWAYS relies on an assumption outside of itself. This symbol could also reasonably

stand for a set. So, we could draw a series of boxes like this ▣ to describe a subset of the first set, and a subset of the subset of the set, and so on. Likewise, we could draw a series of expanding boxes around our original to represent the sets (proofs, truths) that surround and embed

our original like this ▣ . Again, this idea that one proof, one truth, one set of truths necessarily contains a multitude of other (proofs, truths, sets of truths) returns on pages 6 and 7 of NAÏVE SET THEORY. My copy has been heavily, even manically, noted by the original reader. By way of concluding one of his arguments, Halmos admits that

> The set A in this argument was quite arbitrary. We have proved, in other words, that
>
> *nothing contains everything,*

But a second text of the reader's annotations runs parallel to Halmos' argument, clearly marked with precise times indicating when the notes were made. As we read back through these pages, not only can we piece together Halmos' argument, but also reassemble the original reader's progressive comprehension of the argument. So for example, at 7:16 PM on September 14th, 1983, noting the paragraph that appears above, the reader writes

either or nothing head!

just common sense! 9.14.83 7:16

And follows up (at 9:52 PM) with a question   before

realizing (10 minutes later) that we can   Eventually,
by 10:10 PM, the reader has realized the elegance of Halmos' argument

and notes, congratulatorily *[handwritten:]* 0:10 cute ! Halmos follows his assertion
"nothing contains everything" with

or, more spectacularly,

> there is no universe.

           And we get to watch as
the reader comes to grips with that assertion

SEC. 2   **THE AXIOM OF SPECIFICATION**   7

or, more spectacularly,

> there is no universe.

Finally, to state what's already concrete in the writing, reading and noting,
"Universe" here is used in the sense of "universe of discourse," meaning,
in any particular discussion, a set that contains all the objects that enter
into that discussion. *[handwritten:]* 9-14-83 very D+t 7:18 ok!

A SLIGHT PAUSE AS D GATHERS HIMSELF FOR THE CONCLUSION.

Now the talk here this evening, and the printed article when it appears
(in a month or so) on the pages of DOT DOT DOT 17, is also titled

NAÏVE SET THEORY   . As Stuart mentioned, we've
already published an article with the same name by Anthony Huberman
in a previous issue, DOT DOT DOT 15. This is not an accident. Anthony's

article fundamentally deals with the relationship between the amount of information provided about a work of art and the corresponding curiosity that results. He argues that too much information limits the potential power of an artwork and he lays out a number of strategies for stopping the flow of information. His thesis is, roughly speaking, that complete understanding kills any curiosity and produces a dead end. But instead, the ongoing process of attempting to understand (though never really understanding completely) is ABSOLUTELY PRODUCTIVE. The relentless attempt to understand is what keeps a practice moving forward. (I'm pretty certain that William, Kurt and Paul would all agree with Anthony.) Accordingly then, this article both swallows and frames the original article with the same title, providing both a container and a retroactive context for the original.

In what seems like an unavoidable ending, we now return to the Man, the Squirrel and the Tree that they continue to circle and circle around, stuck in an infinite loop with no absolute answer to their metaphysical

question forthcoming . But while they continue to go round and round, I'd like to return to something that I said earlier we'd come back to. You'll remember that William James quoted Søren Kierkegaard as saying

We live forwards,
but we understand backwards.

Well then, THIS IS TO LIVING.

AN AWKWARD SILENCE HANGS FOR APPROX. 15 SECONDS, THEN SUDDEN APPLAUSE.

FOLLOWING THE BREAK, FROM THE RIGHT LECTERN WILL HOLDER READS 2 SHORT EXCERPTS FROM THE LATEST INSTALLMENT-IN-PROGRESS (NOW COMPLETE, BETWEEN PAGES 97–112) OF HIS NOVEL-IN-PROGRESS 'MIDDLE OF NOWHERE'. HE IS SUPPLANTED BY S AT THE LEFT LECTERN.

S : In the previous issue of DOT DOT DOT, Mark Beasley conducted an enlightening interview with Genesis Breyer P-Orridge, whose portrait by Alex Klein is iconically watching over us up there in the corner of the room [gestures over right shoulder] and on the cover of the issue, like some parallel universe Mona Lisa.

In future issues the plan is to continue to publish a series of similar interviews by Mark—and tonight's is with Malcolm McLaren. Apparently Malcolm is performing, or speaking, or doing whatever else he does, elsewhere in London tonight, so we're going to channel him in absentia, through a pre-recorded interview by Mark and his brother Stephen, both also in absentia. I've heard the whole recording, and it's only a slight exaggeration to say the 'interview' consists of a single 'question' followed by Malcolm's two-hour answer. What you're about to hear is a cut-up, achronological edit to fit the allotted thirty minutes. We're going to listen collectively while watching a muted screening of Troma's Californian schlock movie SURFER NAZIS MUST DIE from 1987 sped up three times its original speed to match the length of the interview. The reason for this accompaniment will become apparent. Finally, the Beasleys have asked me to add that the interview is called

sound services JDH Sound

re-recording mixers Mathew Iadarola
Wayne Heitman

mixed in ULTRA-STEREO*

Ultra-Stereo consultants Leo O'Donnell
Jack Cashin

narration John Ayre

radio narration produced by
Young Tom Prod. at
Howietrak Studios, Burbank, CA

STAY TUNED FOR NEWS ON THE "SURF

From SURFER NAZIS MUST DIE (Troma, 1987)

BEASLEY : Having left art school to set up store as a pirate haberdasher on the King's Road, forming and managing the New York Dolls then the Sex Pistols, then more bands, to becoming a band yourself, to making movies, soundtracks, more albums, and audio plays via London, New York, Paris and LA, you returned full circle to producing art using the material you were watching while at art school: the dirty movie ...

MCLAREN : It was natural that eventually, if I wasn't going to be a gallerist and I wasn't going to write about art, I was ultimately going to be cajoled, or seduced, into making art / A young Mexican artist, Stefan Brüggeman, presented me with the word SHALLOW / He was organizing an exhibition with that title and wanted to involve me, presenting something based on that idea / I knew it would be impossible to do something with music, but I wanted very much to have the work dominated by figurative portraits of some kind / I wasn't about to pick up the brush, as I was going to be far too rusty / I just thought in terms of music, which I started to make first / I started to cut up all this music, basically a grab-bag from the annals of pop culture that I had lived through and listened to for decades / We're talking 1950s as a child, 1960s as a teenager, an art student, 1970s doing it, producing it, managing it, selling it, and the 1980s making it myself / I just simply grabbed wholesale samples, huge dollops, of a chorus, or two verses from one song, and stuck it with a chorus from another / I laid down a basic rhythm track, a really generic one I grabbed off a piece of software, and I started to form, to re-invent if you like, these utterly subjective moments in time, my personal taste of what pop culture meant to me / Each particular cut-up revealed the same thing / It was back to that moment when you first heard pop culture, that cry into the wilderness for liberation, which ultimately boiled down to one word, sex / Unbridled unadulterated sex / Sex you never had, only dreamed of, suggested, guessed, looked at, that dirty movies proposed or imagined, but never got / And that hit an idea / I remembered when I was living on baked beans on toast, with a one-kilowatt electric fire, watching dirty movies on 8mm with art students / Movies that suggested all the preamble / This was during the censorship period where you had to at least attempt to show a story before you had people bonking for money / These stories, which were always ill-acted and ill-conceived, so clumsy,

because they were performed by ordinary folk, for fun, for 5, 10, 75, 100 dollars, intrigued me / The amateur nature, the awkwardness, the body language revealed, would be some kind of portrait that I would be interested to align, or at least parallel, with these musical cut-ups / They would exhibit something about the pop culture on the surface / As everybody knows, pop culture will always be interpreted as shallow work, and the gestures of the actors in the dirty movies would equally be considered shallow, insincere, you might say, for sex / I wanted to draw upon those emotions, so I trawled hundreds of films and suddenly realised that I could take these simple portraits, cut out any lip movements to make them appear silent, or at least slowed down, and they would take on a painterly appearance, like silent moving portraits / So I could take a picture of a girl eating a grape before she's about to fuck herself to death, or of a girl nobly walking down a staircase on her way to an orgy, or of four girls in a trailer park waiting for men to partake in their pleasures / Each time it was the moment before sex / That intrigued me / If you just threw them up on the screen and they didn't say anything, would they even suggest sex? / Well, yeah, if you put this music against it, even though you couldn't see any action, couldn't hear anything from the soundtrack, and without any sense of where this material was appropriated from / But they had a kind of elegance, these eerie, uncanny body movements, when the movements were repeated to sustain across the three minute musical cut-up, the length of any particular pop song / So one day I had to go to this downtown gallery in New York / By this time I had seven vignettes and thought I'd just show one / So I showed the first on the reel which was a musical cut-up of The Zombies and Betsy Smith, with a portrait of two people looking at other people having hardcore sex just before they were about to do exactly the same, repeated / Once you slowed it down, you had this feeling it wasn't even repeating / It just had this uncanny quality where although you can't figure out exactly what they're doing, you know something very salacious is going on in the brain, you know there's something sexual / I just loved that idea / And then connecting it to those musical cut-ups, with no rhythmic intention, no being in-sync, gave it a slippery feeling / That disconnect between the music and the image was great, because otherwise they'd fall into that horrible area of being nothing more than a cheap pop video / It had to be constantly disconnected so you'd never feel the two would come together / When I exposed one to these artists, they were so enamoured they asked for more / The gallerist invited me to Art Basel, and I thought, well, seven's not going to be enough, I've got to make it more epic / So I did 21 / Don't asked me why, I just thought that's a magic number / And it was movie time! / I'd finally arrived, after going all the way through the trials and tribulations of Indiana Jones, the offices and studios of Steven Spielberg, wandering the streets of LONDON watching contemporary art exploding with vigour, here I am with actually an art movie / That's it / That's the end, 20 years later / It was the dawn of the Young British Artists / I hung with Tracey Emin, Damien Hirst, and Angela Bulloch / I hung with all those people, and watched and listened and looked / It was extraordinary because the role of contemporary art had changed / Contemporary art was moving into a position where it was embracing all culture, high and low / It had this gargantuan appetite / It seemed, for a moment, as if it was going to be the unquestionable centre of culture rather than hanging in these quite hallowed niches, as it was back in the 1970s / But I didn't understand it, exactly, because they were all doing things I remember going through the process of doing myself, in my own way, throughout the 1970s and 1980s / There were certain pretensions I was querying and questioning that I wasn't certain of / I didn't like the fact that all these artists had PR companies working for them, I couldn't stand the fact that they had managers, that the whole thing was becoming like a business / I think it was because I'd gone through this whole process of throwing myself into a business on a street like the King's Road, with anti-business ethics, and here were artists just wanting to be down and dirty direct business / Business was good, and they were just following these Warhol principles / They were the children of Thatcher, and they were definitely the children of punk, but god, they were soaked in the culture of desire, they wanted stuff, they wanted things to happen, they wanted to be rich / I felt I was connecting to the worst stuff of pop culture / You know why I ended up with the Sex Pistols? / Because they just wanted to be stars and do nothing / I just felt that these new artists, they just wanted fame, fame / At the dawn of the 1990s we were entering into the worst aspects of the culture of desire, which was for everyone to be a celebrity for no matter what / Maybe I was just extremely old-fashioned, I'd soaked up Hollywood, I'd been down and dirty,

and I'd kind of rejected most of it / It was kind of interesting that they were taking on pop-cultural principles and mixing them with some quasi-smattering of borrowed political or subversive thought, but did they truthfully understand or think it through? / No, it was just sort of ... whatever shines brightest / So I didn't fundamentally believe in them too much, but I really appreciated their energy and enthusiasm, and their desire to turn over the art world / They couldn't have come at a better time / You've got this new wave of collectors like Charles Saatchi, who I knew back in the day / He was one of my greatest collectors of pop paraphernalia and memorabilia, particularly records / He'd moved on from collecting old records, but he collected paintings like he collected old records, he bought them wholesale / I particularly remember going with him to a gallery in South London, I think it was the first show of Sarah Lucas at City Racing, and it had all these newspaper works / I thought it was really good, it caught my attention that's for sure, and I think he bought the lot, I thought wow, he's smart, he's good, no question / It had a post-punk element to it, no question / So I nestled in that world a little bit, but didn't really get my feet wet, I didn't really know what to do / I travelled around the world a little bit until the advertising and marketing people picked me up / They drove me insane / That is the worst work in the world, there's nothing more depressing because there's no feedback / They're nothing / It's nothing / Within one year I had to get out, closed that door, and it wasn't long before I returned to the U.S. / I worked on an 'Indiana Jones' film, but not the first one / I came to HOLLYWOOD a little later in the day, 'Temple of Doom' time / I was just one of a selection of Steven's minions whose role it was, at times, when asked, to give your two-penny's worth, to say this, say that, have this idea for music or theme and so on and so forth, sometimes story developments / You were just one of a collection of muses / That's what he did / He liked to have creative people walking through the hallowed rooms of Amblin, which was this special building at the end of the Universal Studios film lot, a kind of fake hacienda with a dog pen, a baby crèche, a jacuzzi, so all those that passed through could park their dog, park their baby, jump in the jacuzzi, talk about story development / It was typical California and Steve's place epitomizes Californian lifestyles / You had these little Aryan-looking blond boys specially cast from UCLA and places, supposedly for security, but if you blew at one they'd drift off like a dandelion leaf / You'd just travel the corridors, pop in and see a screening of one of Steven's favourite movies, 'Lawrence of Arabia', 'Red Shoes', or 'The Third Man' / Steven was obsessed with English movies between the 1940s and 1970s / His favourite director was Michael Powell, who did the first snuff movie, 'Peeping Tom' / Steven didn't just collect us, we were just pawns, little chess pieces, but also bishops and kings, and Michael Powell was one, with the idea that he might have his career resuscitated / He hoped to make a movie but all he ever did was wander the corridors, often with a cane, asking, when am I going to make a movie? / You'd go to collect a cappuccino in the morning and there was this strange guy I didn't know / Sometimes you'd seem to be hallucinating, you'd think, what drugs did I take last night with Jack, where was the club? / So I'd rush back in and talk to one of the girls at the desk asking, Who's that guy in the corridor? / Oh, that's Michael Powell / Oh my god! / And of course six months later he just disappeared, he died / So this is what happened there, people were collected / There were other people like that in Hollywood / They don't do it consciously / It's a way of collecting scripts and their favourite movies, and odd obscure movies that they don't know but someone recommended they should see / So Steven would have this stuff around him, and in Hollywood stuff is people, they collect people like ideas / I was a musical idea, an English eccentric / Ideas that were so foreign to Steven, he liked to have them around and show them off / He'd open the door and there was an idea stuck in the chair, breathing / Malcolm, I want you to meet Harrison / And here he is, Indiana Jones, wow, hi Harrison! / Hi, how you doing ... been listening to that record my wife keeps playing when Steve comes over, we always listen to it, this 'Madame Butterfly', how do you do that? / And Steven would then like me to spin out a tale, because he was equally fascinated / These were the jewels in the crown of Steven's Amblin operation / So that was really the centre, and in a way the most important position I ever held in the bowels of Hollywood / Then I found my way back to Europe just as that ship was trying to leave King's road in the form of the World's End / Just as that archaeological dig in St. Christopher's place, Nostalgia of Mud was taking place / Just as those hobos were washing and walking round the King's Road / 'Buffalo Girls' was playing over the airwaves / I was equally part of that journey and I happened to park my butt, not by design but by sheer accident, in LA on a promotional trip, and for whatever reason suddenly got terribly ill / It wasn't food poisoning, more a kind of tiredness, a flu of some kind / I was ensconced in a hotel on Sunset Boulevard and the record company forgot about me! / Three weeks later I started to appear out of bed in these corridors, and for some reason this hotel, which was brand new then, on Sunset Boulevard, was a real stop, a trend spot, and I kept getting noticed / People would ask me, are you Malcolm McLaren, and I would say yeah / Wow, so great to meet you! / Then a day later I'd get these calls from film studios / Would you like to come to a meeting? / We would love to have a meeting with you, could you put it in your diary? / Could you come to the studio? / Do we need to send a car for you? / That's how I literally took one meeting, with no real intention of taking a job, then at the end the guy says, well Malcolm, whaddya think ... you could be drinking champagne here on Monday morning with a nice big fat cheque and an agent to help you look for a house / I think you're going to be a good asset at this film studio / Do you have any ideas for musical films? / I never particularly adored the exercise of scriptwriting / I always found it very difficult, simply because you always had to dig very deep into narrative and I wasn't trained to do narrative / The work I embraced in art school was outside all that, actually the opposite, non-narrative, and scriptwriting was far too disciplined and literary- rather than visually-driven for me / I was interested more in the art end, or the pop end, of movie making, and the bit in between felt very ugly and heavy / But these people are extraordinarily persuasive / It was the whole thing, the big fat cheque, the champagne, and I was lost in LA, the record company had just left me by the roadside, in decent conditions but still the roadside, I'd just finished making 'Madame Butterfly' and getting through it was hell I didn't really know what I wanted to do, I think if someone had told me I was now an artist I would have fallen back into the art world / I'd only been there a week or two and so I thought, oh well, maybe I should try this out, you know, fate plays you a card and, hey, let's open this door and see what's in here / So that Monday morning I arrived for work / That was it, I was there, there was the desk and the secretary, you've got to meet your estate agent at 4pm but first you need a coffee / I'm a pretty decent storyteller, but the actual discipline of writing a screenplay is really something / You can't just pick it up, you really just need to read a lot of screenplays, and they really are the most horrible cack-handed, literary things / You've got to read what the weather is first, and what this guy's going to say, and this is where he's positioned / Did we have a script for 'The Great Rock & Roll Swindle'? / No, we did it on the spot / Each morning I would write for that day / I had, in a way, constructed this strange ad hoc script, which was basically, I'm going to give you the ten lessons, like the ten commandments, on how to swindle your way to the top, and in these Ten Commandments I'm going to relate the history of the Sex Pistols / This other stuff that I was given in Hollywood was really much more difficult / I found it really, really hard / I used to nod off and they used to say, Malcolm doesn't have much attention span / So in the end I actually thought, fuck it, I can't read this script, so I'd sit down and write titles / I was very good at titles, and I came up with this one: HEAVY METAL SURFING NAZIS / So I went into this boardroom meeting where everybody has to throw their ideas around / It was Monday morning and that's what you do: you throw your ideas around till lunchtime / Anyway, and it came to my turn to pitch, this new guy on the block, what's he got? / And I said, I just got a title ... I think surfing could be re-invented in musical terms / I'd been listening to Dick Dale and all this surfing guitar music / I think surfing could have another dusting down, a revival / Great idea! Great idea! What do you think, Harry? What else? What else you got, Malcolm? / I just got this title, 'Heavy Metal Surfing Nazis' / Wow! That's big! It sounds big / I said, yeah ... the idea is to get a heavy metal surfing movie, with the guitars, the drums / I'm thinking big, thinking gangs, nasty, tough, hardcore guys, you know, people fighting for the waves / Got it, Malcolm! Got it! We got to think creative now ... who's going to write it? Who's going to write it? We'll come back to you, Malcolm, great, keep it up! / So I went back to my office very happy / After two or three weeks, the same guy says, Malcolm, been talking about this all week, this surfing idea of yours, you gotta understand, we can't have that ... I think we gotta drop the last word / And he says, 'Heavy Metal Surfers', we like that, just 'Heavy Metal Surfers' / And I said, no, no, no ... it doesn't have the same ring ... we need 'Nazis' on the end, that's what gives it the bite / I can't do that, Malcolm ... you know, punk rock, it's over ... that was back in London, okay? Cut the Nazi shit ... 'Heavy Metal Surfers', okay? / Back to desk, another week passed, we met a few writers, this guy, that guy, went back into the room, he says, Malcolm, how's it all going? / I said, well, we'll bring you some scripts, got you some writers here / Good, good, good, but hey, we still been talking about this, we can't get over it, you know ... surfing musical is fantastic, but you're right, you're damn right, 'Heavy Metal Surfers' just doesn't do it for me either ... after several meetings and thinking about it this week we all agree, we got another idea, Malcolm, and we think you're gonna love it ... go on, tell him Harry, what did ya come up with? / And Harry says, 'Surfer's Fantasy'! / I say, what? / 'Surfer's Fantasy'! This is something else, we like it, it's got imagination, we think it's nice, it's romantic, Malcolm, think about it, trust us, we got years of experience here ... 'Surfer's Fantasy', that's great, we could do at least 500 theatres, probably a thousand ... go work on it, boy, it's gonna be good / So I went back to my office and I thought, gee, from 'Heavy Metal Surfing Nazis' to 'Surfer's Fantasy' and it's just the title were talking about / I didn't get any further than just that one line of the script and we ended up with 'Surfer's Fantasy' / That's a Hollywood tale / So, you know, I went through many of those kinds of journeys with different people, even with Steven I have to say, and learned a lot, got depressed a lot, and realised you can't be too creative, too conceptual, in Hollywood, it just doesn't work / I realised that after a time, after four years, and I eventually I went back to Europe without ever making a movie / And they used to say, don't get depressed, Malcolm, do you play tennis, hey, we're having a barbeque, come and meet the wife, listen, Malcolm, its okay, hey, I used to be an insurance broker, got into scriptwriting, moved the family out here, haven't made a movie, but I'm doing some fine living, great wife, good children, nice house, you'll learn to love it here / C'mon lets play some tennis, that was the life, that's LA / People actually continued there with no problem, wandering around, never actually achieving anything, but nevertheless being paid to not achieve anything / I realised then I was an artist, I couldn't do this, I didn't need the wife, I didn't need the house / I cut out / I cut out and came back to Europe.

DURING THE FINAL BREAK A LARGE PRINT IS PLACED ON THE EASEL. ON RETURNING, S IS BEHIND THE LEFT LECTERN, D BEHIND THE RIGHT ONE (WHICH IS TURNED TO FACE THE AUDIENCE AND HOLDS 2 HARDBACK NOVELS, ONE RED, ONE GREEN), AND WILL HOLDER LAYS ON THE FLOOR BETWEEN THEM. D SPEAKS.

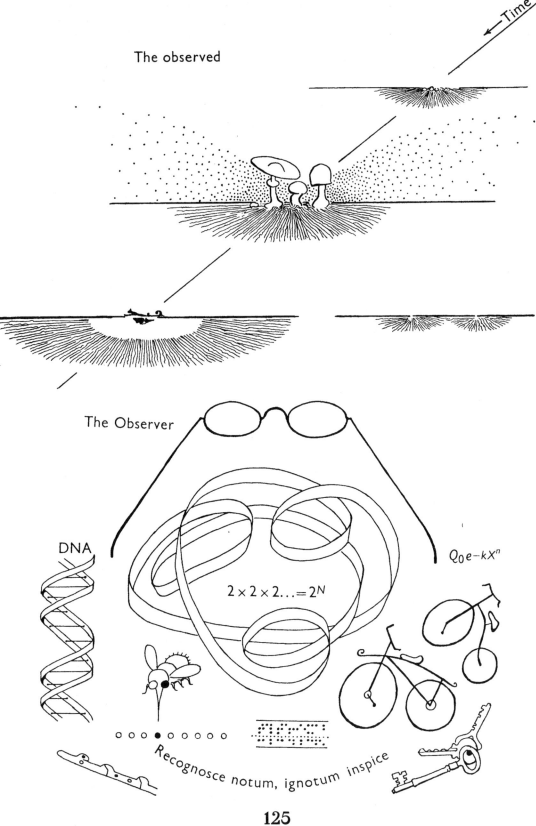

The observed

← Time

The Observer

DNA

$Q_0 e - kX^n$

$2 \times 2 \times 2 \ldots = 2^N$

Recognosce notum, ignotum inspice

D: Stuart will now give the last talk, the title of which is SCIENCE, FICTION, written SCIENCE COMMA FICTION—with syntax-breaking punctuation which defies accurate translation to speech. As should have become apparent by now, the impossibility of translation from the written to the spoken—and vice versa—has been central to the past three evenings and future 144 pages we're presently about to conclude.

So, Stuart …

S : This piece is being read to inaugurate the republication by Hyphen Press of E.C. Large's first two novels, 'Sugar in the Air' and 'Asleep in the Afternoon', which have been out of print since the end of the 1930s. As my title suggests, Large was a scientist—an industrial chemist and plant pathologist—as well as a writer, and the image to my left is one he drew himself to accompany a piece in a scientific journal, which embodies the breadth of his interests.

As you may know, we've been cannibalizing and republishing fragments of Large's writing for a while now, including an entire chapter in DOT DOT DOT 15. Hopefully this has begun to provoke the kind of interest and audience we think Large deserves. Alongside the novels, Robin Kinross and myself have also prepared a third supplementary book, 'God's Amateur', which collects a number of Large's shorter pieces written for various literary journals, mostly in the years leading up to these novels. This third book also contains a short biographical note by Robin, and the essay I'm going to read tonight with a little help from Will and David.

If you read the first piece in issue 15—an opening chapter transplanted from 'Asleep in the Afternoon'—you may recall that it begins with the protagonist C.R. Pry laid on the floor exercising a peculiarly British form of existentialism: he refuses to do anything after lunch but attempt to sleep until he can think of something he really wants to do, in mute protest against the various hobbies, pottering and pastimes expected of him. In homage to this scene, Will will read all the E.C. Large excerpts laid on his back on the floor, while David will read all other quotes from the other lectern. He begins with the standard definition of Scientific Method as a general preface, then I'll read my account of Large's SCIENCE, FICTION.

SCIENTIFIC METHOD:
1. DEFINE THE QUESTION
2. GATHER INFORMATION & RESOURCES
3. FORM HYPOTHESIS
4. PERFORM EXPERIMENT & COLLECT DATA
5. ANALYZE DATA
6. INTERPRET DATA & DRAW CONCLUSIONS THAT SERVE AS A STARTING POINT FOR NEW HYPOTHESES
7. PUBLISH RESULTS

Ideally this essay will be spoken with deceptive ease—or at least something akin to the casual dedication in Large's second novel:

To E.H. over a bottle of wine

In other words, it should embody the steady spirit of its subject, a writer who was always chasing the underlying, irreducible truth of each new situation. Both E.C. Large and his fictional double C.R. Pry are driven (not to say condemned) by the need to seek out the root causes of local defects—"what exactly is going on here?"—and the shortcomings that need to be exposed are usually social ones. Such self-discipline is manifest in Large's ragged hand- and typewritten manuscripts, the understated precision and protracted pace of which are already lost to another generation. They are fossils of a practical decorum which has been abandoned, perhaps irretrievably, along with the wider implications of civility beyond language, by which I suppose I simply mean 'good manners'. They also convey a distinct sense of practice; that is, plainly PRACTISING WRITING TO GET BETTER AT IT rather than some grander calling to THE PRACTICE OF WRITING—and in Large's case the proletarian overtones of 'writer' resonate more convincingly than the pretensions of 'author', as he implies himself:

He set out the typewriter, the manuscript, the paper and his several mechanical aids to production, on his table, as though he were going to be timed for typewriting under the Bedaux system, but he did not yet start. Forty days and forty nights! Five hundred and sixty-one pages in that stack of manuscript four inches high … Even so, the typescript-production graph had still to be prepared. On this graph pages of typescript were to be plotted against the pages of manuscript. An ideal line on the graph showed how many pages of typescript there should be when he had reached any given page of the manuscript, if he was going to end up with exactly four hundred typed pages …

My copy of Large's fourth and final book 'Dawn in Andromeda' arrived in the mail with an auspicious photograph glued to the inside of its cover: the writer apparently at work on the manuscript of the same book, sat behind

E.C. Large, 1956

a makeshift table at the end of a garden with a pile of what appear to be encyclopaedias or dictionaries. According to an obituary note the picture was probably taken on a Sunday morning, and this casual snapshot of the weekend writer implies two ideas which are not necessarily contradictory—that for Large writing was a pleasant pastime, but also one urgent enough to occupy what was then still upheld as a traditional (ie. religious) day of leisure. This is not lower-case work in the sense of labour, but capitalized Work in the sense of artistry; a NECESSARY HOBBY, then, with as much allusion to compulsion, of being held in a grip, as to the fix of creation. The personal and communal dilemmas that arise from this conflict form the basis of Large's first two novels, 'Sugar in the Air' and 'Asleep in the Afternoon', and given their largely autobiographical content it is clear that Large simply—constitutionally—HAD TO WRITE. This urgency, which only occasionally slides into desperation, is at the root of both novels' recurring motif: the struggle to 'win back' time from industry, the staking of a claim to LIVE life rather than spend it occupied by the drudgery of labour, manual or otherwise. The elliptical fact that for Large this 'living' was practically synonymous with 'writing' (at least at the time these first books were written, as well as during the timeframe WITHIN the novels) is typical of the looping self-reflexivity that propels it.

DOUBLE BIND

'Sugar in the Air' is a story of the cycle of an idea. In this case the biological one compressed into its deadpan title—a novel's 'only line of poetry' according to Large (speaking in character). Charles Pry is a chemical engineer fast approaching the end of two years' self-imposed unemployment spent trying to write, who unwittingly finds himself directing an improbable attempt to produce glucose from carbon dioxide. To the surprise of all involved, not least himself, Pry's experiments succeed. He establishes a commercially viable factory, then involves himself in all aspects of its production, incrementally establishing the soundness and success of its product Sunsap, which is eventually processed into useful cattle feed. Pry then continues to manage the company long enough to observe—with public detachment and private dismay—its hapless board of directors dismantle the entire project. The decline is as rapid and reckless as its progress was slow and careful, a domino effect

of conflicting vested interests in which the frequently infantile logic of industrial capitalism comes across as both easily avoidable and depressingly inevitable. By the close of the novel both Pry's factory and ambition have shut down, and he is precisely back where he began, having secured enough profit from the venture to support himself without work for a further couple of years.

Had Large stopped there he would have left a debut whose first impression as a rudimentary portrait of inter-war industrial relations reveals itself on closer inspection to be more concerned with scrutinizing the human ones underneath. Large carefully inscribed a double layer into the novel through a cast of caricatures (mad scientist, tyrannical director, jealous colleague, etc., with Pry playing the human being) who are at once TOO BLATANTLY clichéd to come across as mere realism, and TOO VIVIDLY drawn from life to come across as mere parody. 'Sugar in the Air''s default temper is sardonic and satirical, but both Large and Pry, author and protagonist, care too much DESPITE THEMSELVES to come across as one-dimensionally bitter. Pry is more complex a character than the so-called angry young men who would soon populate postwar English fiction, being essentially an articulation of inward deliberation rather than outward bravado, marked by the constant struggle to identify, understand and come to terms with his own fundamentally contradictory impulses. This self-doubt is the core of Large's writing ("at its best in its helplessness", as he once reflected) and tragicomically manifest in the gap between his straightforward no-nonsense depiction of the anything-but-straightforward nonsense of human relations.

By similar oppositional design, Large painted his social backdrop deliberately larger than life, so conspicuously 'of its time' that the novel's more timeless aspects—its attitudes—are offset in greater relief. In other words, the false scenery is patently detachable (therefore transposable) and such technical doublethink is both central to the novel's effect and one of its key themes. Picking at the details of what Pry christens 'nominal democracy'—EVERYTHING DONE IN THE NAME OF SOMETHING ELSE—Large repeatedly attempts to reach beyond this surface to essence. In fact, this extract from one of his shorter journal pieces might easily double as blurb for 'Sugar in the Air''s dust jacket:

> About Socialism, about Communism, Pacifism, Capitalism, yes, but something more than the mere reshuffling of the jargon

of Socialist theory. The tags used, because for some they are terms of reference, but the search always into the contents of these parcels, not the tags.[1]

These contents are his characters' beliefs, conceits and motivations; WAYS OF THINKING articulated at the level of everyday interactions, not yet hardened enough to qualify as bona fide (theoretical, polemical) PHILOSOPHIES, and so more practicable: easy to relate, and to relate to.

But Large didn't stop there; instead he wrote a sequel, or a meta-sequel. Hardly pausing for breath and barely bothering to re-introduce the cast, 'Asleep in the Afternoon' picks up exactly where 'Sugar in the Air' left off, then proceeds to continue, duplicate, and mirror it all at once. As such, the sequel is also about the cycle of an idea, only this time a literary rather than scientific one. Instead of managing a factory, Pry writes a novel—also called 'Asleep in the Afternoon'—whose own progress is related through various summaries, paraphrases or entire chapters embedded in the outer story. 'Asleep in the Afternoon' quickly bifurcates into two stories, with Pry's 'real' experiences increasingly informing those of his characters —and ultimately, of course, a third once the reader realizes that Pry's writing 'Asleep in the Afternoon' is itself a more or less biographical account of Large's writing 'Sugar in the Air'.

Setting into motion another snake-eating-its-own-tail, Large concludes his second novel with Pry's first being published and acclaimed, along with enough advance royalties and promise of a literary career to avoid the permanent threat of a 'return to industry'. Both books follow an identical looping trajectory from a state of mental and physical inertia, through a period of passion, activity and enlightenment, then back to the former state, a sense of resignation and only the merest glimmer of satisfaction at having 'used' the time creatively. The books themselves—both fictional and actual—are now monuments to this oasis of economic 'freedom', two years frozen in abstract form of text-as-thought and physical form of book-as-object.

It is a platitude that debut novels frequently involve protagonists who are thinly-veiled versions of their authors, and one good reason for avoiding re-presentation of Large through narrative biography here is because the essential aspects of both stories are based on Large's own life, with little attempt to disguise it. Like Pry, Large worked as a chemical engineer (making 'Sulsol' rather than 'Sunsap') before being able to support himself briefly as a writer, and likewise found himself at the end of both books faced with the tenuous promise of a literary career conditional on adequate sales.

LOW MODERNISM

My wish here is to insist that 'Sugar in the Air' and 'Asleep in the Afternoon' ought to be considered a single piece of work. To ignore one or the other is to miss much more than half the story, the depth of Large's art and the breadth of his work's inherent ambition.

With the slightest hint of derision Large opens 'Sugar in the Air' with Pry "trying to write a book, a treatise", an introductory glimpse of the self-awareness that will intermittently descend into self-loathing. Here Large reflects his context not only by describing his surroundings, but by practising and—crucially—OBSERVING THE PRACTICE OF PRACTISING the self-consciousness typical of modernist literature of the surrounding decades. For years I've claimed that one reason for republishing Large is that his self-reflexivity was ahead of its time, but on reflection this claim doesn't actually hold up too well considering the lineage of involuted fiction that predates it. This stems from Sterne's 'Tristram Shandy' (arguably further back to Rabelais or even Cervantes) then on to Joyce and Beckett, their German-writing contemporaries such as Musil and Walser, and later stretching on to writers as diverse as Borges, Nabokov and Calvino. This branch of literary modernism ran roughly parallel to the 'heroic' phase of twentieth century art and architecture, similarly liberated by formal experiment and the exposure of underlying mechanics. Its proponents worked towards a literature founded on progressive realism (more simply—and problematically—under the banner of 'truth') as opposed to the supposedly stagnant presence of the bourgeois Romantic narrative.

The quality that sets Large's writing apart from these broad contemporaries, however, is essentially anti-literary: his novels (particularly) are grounded. Although technically sophisticated, they don't SEEM to be. While the writing is consistently austere it remains generous, buoyed against its regular pockets of claustrophobia and desperation by a solemn kind of joy and stubborn, if still half-ashamed, independence. Take Pry's autobiographical vignette, delivered here to Sunsap's board of directors, who regard him almost fondly as an eccentric irritant:

"If you will consult your records you will find how long I have been with this company. Before that I was technical manager of a breakfast food company in Durham. My initials are C.R., I enjoy good health, I am punctual and industrious, and of temperate habits. I have no morals, no principles and no politics."

Next to the show-offishness of the modernist canon (Joyce as stylistic virtuoso, Beckett as minimal extremist, Borges as byzantine fantasist, Nabokov as shadow puppeteer, etc.) Large's debut novels are, then, unassuming. The tone, manner and trajectory of Large's narration is straight-faced, precise and plodding—qualities which might amount to a dour 'scientific' demeanour if not so regularly checked by self-deprecation and a tendency to daydream. In fact, Large writes with such alacrity that his approach might more accurately be considered 'low' in relation to the more cerebral, propulsive 'high' modernists, and suggests why his reputation fell quickly below the critical radar. Large shares something of the stereotypical British modesty and resolute smallness of such as G.K. Chesterton (astute observation and local pragmatism) or Henry Green (the mores of particular social pockets), but 'Sugar in the Air' and 'Asleep in the Afternoon' fall most comfortably in line with Robert Tressell's socialist tract-novel 'The Ragged Trousered Philanthropists' (1914), whose righteous everyman Frank Owen might be considered a blueprint of Pry in an age before irony, only a quarter of a century earlier.

While in retrospect Large's directness might be considered an alternative to—or relief from—the asceticism of higher-brow Continental modernism, the British critics of 1938 found 'Asleep in the Afternoon''s cleverness reprehensible, another characteristically British attitude which has since dogged a strain of self-reflexive British writers such as B.S. Johnson and Alasdair Gray. Johnson's 'Albert Angelo' (1964) was the first of a sequence of what he called autobiographical novels, founded on the staunch precept that "telling stories is telling lies" and whose narrative accordingly breaks down into an "almighty apotheosis" of stark self-criticism. Although critical reception to Johnson's work was uneven (but by no means predominantly negative) to Johnson's mind he was always pejoratively labelled "experimental", a term he came to categorically reject. Gray's compulsive Glaswegian odyssey 'Lanark' (1981), on the other hand, employs baroque appendages of self-parody (notes, asides, appendices and

typographic play) which have been consistently read as a security device deliberately set to anticipate and defuse external criticism; a claim which grows increasingly vertiginous when some of the critics of this device also appear to have been invented by Gray himself.

The novels of Large, Johnson and Gray have little in common, either stylistically or thematically, yet it seems to me they have all ostensibly arrived at a similar point of artistic involution through serious, candid reflection. Their mutual commitment to an idea(l) of honesty—and the various formal solutions it has contrived—is rooted in a shared attempt at literary transparency whose intentions and implications are both personal and social.

This distinctly local breed of involution defines another overlooked piece of British reflexivity: Lindsay Anderson's feature film 'O Lucky Man!' (1973) is a three-hour anti-epic which follows its cartoonish naïve-idealist Michael Travis (played by Malcolm McDowell) around England, its scenes partly written in transit between shooting. In an extended closing sequence Travis, lost in an evening crowd at Oxford Circus, happens upon a sign—"Try your luck!"—and is directed into an open film audition populated by the rest of the cast of the same film the viewer is just about to finish watching, as well as Anderson the director playing himself in charge of its casting. When Travis is pulled from the crowd for a screen test, Anderson closes in and repeatedly asks him to smile for the camera. He refuses a number of times, then—in an apparent epiphany—his confused, indignant frown starts to reverse and the camera cuts. The film effectively ends on this ambiguity I have since come to interpret as: ONLY LAUGHTER COULD STEEL HIM IN HIS NEW AWARENESS.

Just as the art of Pry reflects the life of Large, and vice versa, this scene mirrors Malcolm McDowell's first actual audition for the director, which resulted in their earlier collaboration 'If...' (to which 'O Lucky Man!' can reasonably be considered a sequel). Anderson also worked in the same reflexive territory as a number of continental European counterparts, most obviously the French New Wave, yet—again like Large—departs from them where the work-turning-in-on-itself seems less the knowing gesture of an intellectual auteur invested in the history of cinema, and more an intuitive solution to a 'technical' problem encountered during the writing: how to offset a layer of meaning—the politics of transparency—drawn FROM the subject rather than applied TO it.

During my most recent re-reading of Large's novels, I had the uncomfortable feeling that my attraction to all this arch self-awareness of such as Large's art was merely a matter of taste (like preferring red to green). This bothered me inasmuch as I had previously assumed the self-reflexivity carried some kind of critical, moral or ethical weight—a conviction which seemed suddenly groundless, or at best too oblique to be philosophically practicable. The more I considered it, the less I was able to hold the idea in focus, and it was some time before the itch was scratched by another anecdote to another introduction to another classic work of involution, the extensively annotated version of Nabokov's 'Lolita', as compiled by Alfred Appel, Jr., worth quoting at length here:

> One afternoon my wife and I built a puppet theatre. After propping the theatre on the top edge of the living room couch, I crouched down behind it and began manipulating the two hand puppets in the stage above me. The couch and the theatre's scenery provided good cover, enabling me to peer over the edge and watch the children immediately become engrossed in the show, and then virtually mesmerized by my improvised little story that ended with a patient father spanking an impossible child. But the puppeteer, carried away by his story's violent climax, knocked over the entire theatre, which clattered onto the floor, collapsing in a heap of cardboard, wood and cloth—leaving me crouched, peeking out at the room, my head now visible over the couch's rim, my puppeted hands, with their naked wrists, poised in mid-air. For several moments my children remained in their open-mouthed trance, still in the story, staring at the space where the theatre had been, not seeing me at all. Then they did the kind of double-take that a comedian might take a lifetime to perfect, and began to laugh uncontrollably, in a way I had never seen before—and not so much at my clumsiness, which was nothing new, but rather at those moments of total involvement in a non-existent world, and at what its collapse implied to them about the authenticity of the larger world, and about their daily efforts to order it and their own fabricated illusions. They were laughing, too, over their sense of what the vigorous performance had meant to me; but they saw how easily they could be tricked and their trust belied, and the shrillness of their laughter finally suggested that they recognized the frightening implications of what had happened, and that only laughter could steel them in their new awareness.[2]

EXPERIENCE AND CONVENIENCE

Reflection might be Large's (Pry's) defining quality, but his self-criticism is rarely wasted. Rather than wallow in his insight he USES it, as one critic noted: "Mr Pry was quite a man, though I don't recall the author's saying so ... He is no hero but he gets things done." Pry's rite of passage through 'Sugar in the Air' is mirrored in a recurring conversation with his appointed mentor, Professor Zaareb, who repeatedly chastises his occasional egoistic preoccupations with short term success (generally comic lapses into vanity, materiality, or delusions of grandeur). Zaareb's mature, if not exactly zen, priorities are, by comparison, always 'for science', which is to say broad cultural progress and collective enlightenment rather than immediate local benefit and personal gain.

> "You young men never see that Research is a cultural pursuit: you wouldn't expect Big Business to pay you for writing poems or having music lessons, would you?"

At the beginning of their working relationship Pry interprets Zaareb's attitude as plain arrogance, but when he hesitates during the patenting—the public dispersion—of their research and Zaareb demands:

> "You pretend to want to give your work to the world, don't you? Now that you are forced to do so, what cause have you to complain?"

A humbled Pry replies:

> "I am beginning to feel, Dr. Zaareb, that my real reward in all this is the privilege of association with people like you."

This exchange marks the end of Pry's professional adolescence—in part through the new realization that Zaareb's disinterest is a safety valve against hubris. And if this new realization of his work as a social rather than a personal project destroys some of its intense appeal (or 'love'), the same detachment insulates him against the destructive actions of the board of capitalists. As they plough through one slapstick decision after another, systematically unravelling the immediate practical results of Pry's two years' labour, his wider contribution to scientific knowledge remains immune.

Large's push towards a form of literary transparency can be read as a form of personal (and, crucially, personally-arrived-at) resistance to prevailing forms of government and other social management. That its righteous independence seems so pertinent seventy years on is a reflection of how the 'nominal democracy' Pry solemnly regards has only gained momentum since, towards a critical mass now defined (in modern Western society at least) by ubiquitous spin doctoring, the widespread distrust of government, and the resultant gulf between any state and the public it contrives to represent. In short, a collective resignation to the failure of democracy, or at (the very) least to lingering socialist notions of it.

At the turn of the century in his survey of 'The Nineties' (2001) the cultural critic Michael Bracewell portrayed immediate history as a total inversion of Large's ideals. Contrary to Large's 1930s drive to get 'beyond surface to essence', Bracewell's Nineties stall at the subtitle: 'When Surface was Depth'. In this scenario culture has been reduced to a number of familiar codes: infantilism, chauvinism, retroactive reference and militantly manufactured 'authenticity'—all packaged through a 'comedy of recognition', contained by ubiquitous quotation marks at least a step removed from any founding 'reality'. This is the logical, tragic outcome of Large's 'nominal democracy', with experience supplanted IN THE NAME OF SOMETHING ELSE: convenience.

"The end result of these ideas", Bracewell concludes, "would be the feeling that, we, the consumer democracy, were in fact POST-POLITICAL—and afflicted with a Fear of Subjectivity." The germ of this condition was already permeating 'Asleep in the Afternoon' some sixty years earlier—in the following passage, for example, where Pry gently mocks the 'convenience' of the book club which recommends his own novel as 'book of the month':

> Wonderful! No routing about in second-hand book shops; no venturing and searching for themselves; no counting the money in their pockets before plunging on a book they had slowly come to desire. No carrying the coveted book home, under their coat, hiding it from Mary or saying it cost rather less than it did, half ashamed of the extravagance, when it could have been read for nothing, sooner or later, at the British Museum. No looking over their shelves and seeing how their taste and understanding had grown with the years. No sense that the choice of books was like the choice of friends. Perhaps they had their friends, and maybe also their concubines, chosen for them by a selection committee. What a lot of trouble it saved.

Large repeatedly draws attention to this loss of experience in the face of convenience, and

invokes the corollary 'convenience' of hollow political rhetoric versus the 'experience' of quantifiable and verifiable facts. His own prose is accordingly artless, stripped of affectation, its voice a familiar, even-tempered common denominator. The usually reticent Pry even finds himself heckling a speaker on the subject in 'Asleep in the Afternoon':

> "The contradiction to which the bourgeois speaker draws attention is dialectical and inevitable under capitalism."
> There was a murmur of approval; the meeting seemed to find this answer completely satisfactory.
> "That is so much cant," said Pry, "and one useful way of preserving culture is to speak plain English."

Pry's call for common language here is supported by Large's example, writing the scene specifically and economically himself, casting out "about half the present vocabulary of politicians, clerics, philosophers, economists and others afflicted with proselytizing zeal". In a contemporaneous book review (of 'The Tyranny Of Words' for the 'New English Weekly') he promotes such semantic discipline by trawling various examples of overblown rhetoric and censoring each redundant word with a pragmatic "BLAB" to emphasize the point.[3]

CLASSIC ROMANTIC

Large's writing is rife with multiple meanings, carefully crafted for the close reader whose assumed absence is but one aspect of his artistic melancholy: "two or three people in a thousand would taste it, and it would warm the cockles of their crapulous hearts", acknowledges Pry with a kind of bitter, self-preserving glee when 'explaining' the poetry of 'Asleep in the Afternoon''s title to Mary. "All the rest might think it wholly sweet and delightful ...". Large's chapter headings alone are rife with double and triple entendres, but the novels' shared subtitle, 'A Romance' is more prominent and allusive than most for a number of reasons.

First, because the tone and stance of both books are consistently—romantically—against all odds, their very publication barely believed by Large himself as some miracle combination of trial, error, good fortune and timing. Second, with regard to the fact that the definition of romance as 'ARDENT EMOTIONAL ATTACHMENT OR INVOLVEMENT BETWEEN TWO PEOPLE' could be rewritten as '... BETWEEN A PERSON AND HIS WORK' to describe Large's (Pry's) professional temperament—or equally, '... BETWEEN AN AUTHOR AND HIS READER', for that matter. Third, because of the constant sense of his trespassing on a foreign discipline, romantically spending (or wasting) time and effort on an activity without immediate or obvious gain, and most regularly justified to himself as a debt owed in lieu of time lost to prolonged study and forced labour. Fourth, with regard to that essential uselessness of writing which affords it ironic agency, manipulating the ills of marriage, industry, government and religion into art—the romantic distillation of sugary life from dead air.

But above all because of the audacity with which Large slips his contrariness past the reader (on the title page!) by assuming the guise of conventional scene-characters-plot Romantic novels—which they ARE, in part; but they use rather than embody the form, and the distinction is critical. 'Sugar in the Air' is a straightforward indictment of industrial capitalism and its attendant envy, greed and avarice, while 'Asleep in the Afternoon' admonishes a public contentedly dormant on the eve of war. Ultimately, Pry (Large) is resigned to the deeper causes of both circumstances, and takes only the flimsiest, most suspicious comfort in the apparent dignity of his art as a personal stand (or coping device). Another critic portrayed him as being

> so competent in his work and dedicated to it and personally decent, in short so expressive of the qualities we demand of any proper citizen, that he has no time or thought for self-advertising and thrusting and bald advancement and front, and is thus naturally put out like garbage in the end, the pure damn fool.[4]

As an overview of Large's four published books, 'Sugar in the Air' (1937) is a piece of fiction about science, 'Asleep in the Afternoon' (1938) is fiction about the science of writing fiction, 'The Advance of the Fungi' (1940) is a history of science with the tone of fiction, and 'Dawn in Andromeda' (1957) is 'pure' science fiction (which is to say that for the first time it adheres to the conventions of a genre and is less inspired for doing so). Again, this cross-pollination of approaches, voices and genres from Large's various careers seems to be rooted in Large's autodidactic discipline, the constant flexing and toning of a literary muscle.

We leave Pry at the close of 'Asleep in the Afternoon', his 'book of the month' a confirmed best-seller, considering a return to science and an adventure involving organic micro-cultures rather than London's literary culture. Having dutifully trawled his own reviews with amusement and breezily observed the dismantling of his book's window display, the folly of writing seems adequately drained from our anti-hero's system—he is suddenly prepared for a profession instead of a romance. And so Pry's circular existence starts over, once again mirroring Large's actual circumstances. The poor commercial and critical reception of 'Asleep in the Afternoon' appears to have extinguished the chance of his shorter non-fiction being published. In any case, the Second World War intervened, and Large's next major undertaking—analysis of a national potato blight—was to "save his life": agricultural research was acceptable war work for a sworn Pacifist.

While it seems that, professionally at least, Large never really reconciled the division of his scientific and literary work, it is precisely the symbiosis of the two that animates his early fiction today. His writing is defined by a wide-ranging set of interests, temperament and capacity which is equal parts classic and romantic—a duality which extends to any of the parallel dichotomies itemized by Robert M. Pirsig in his 'Zen and the Art of Motorcycle Maintenance': Scientific vs. Artistic, Technical vs. Human, or Rational vs. Emotional. Pirsig sets up these opposites in order to assert that the fundamental misunderstanding, disinformation, mistrust and hostility which characterizes modern societies are rooted in the personal and communal inability to reconcile these two poles:

> Persons tend to think and feel exclusively in one mode or the other and in doing so tend to misunderstand and underestimate what the other mode is all about. But no one is willing to give up the truth as he sees it, and as far as I know, no one now living has any real reconciliation of these truths or modes. There is no point at which these visions of reality are unified.[5]

Large's body of work is radical and instructive precisely because it covers all bases. His output ranges from the early reveries and reviews, through political commentary on topical issues (air raid shelters, conscription, propaganda), the domestic concerns of the family home and his 'Wind and Wandering' travelogues, through to later papers on plant pathology. Whether 'About the working class' or 'The control of potato blight', all are afforded the same serious consideration, dissected with impartial intellect, and the 'findings' articulated through the bricks-and-mortar construction of pragmatic argument.

*

The careful ceremony of dismantling and reassembling the typewriter; the graphs which variously chart the novels' progression and diminishing bank savings; the writer's block, analyzed, diagnosed, treated and resolved within the space of a single chapter; and the vertiginous craft with which the wife's knowing-her-husband-better-than-he-knows-himself is captured by necessarily knowing HER a step better yet in order to portray it—all are vignettes drawn simultaneously from Large's and Pry's life and fiction which describe the unique disposition of the scientist-writer. Yet none are quite as succinct as his anticipation of the deft Möbius Strip of 'Asleep in the Afternoon''s design:

IN A YEAR I SHOULD PASS THROUGH A RICH VARIETY OF MOODS

∴ SO WOULD THE BOOK

∴ IN THAT AT LEAST IT WOULD HAVE SOME VERISIMILITUDE TO LIFE

Thanks for listening. ∎

NOTES
1. 'Hail!', in Stuart Bailey & Robin Kinross (eds.), in 'God's Amateur: The Writing of E.C. Large', London: Hyphen, 2008.
2. Alfred Appel, Jr., 'The Annotated Lolita' [revised edition, 1991], London: Penguin Books, 1995.
3. 'The semantic discipline', in Stuart Bailey & Robin Kinross (eds.), in 'God's Amateur: The Writing of E.C. Large', London: Hyphen, 2008.
4. Otis Ferguson, 'One for the reader' (review of 'Sugar in the Air'), in 'The New Republic', 8 September 1937.
5. Robert M. Pirsig, 'Zen and the Art of Motorcycle Maintenance' [1974], New York: Bantam Books, 1981.

APPLAUSE. WILL GETS UP FROM THE FLOOR AND JOINS THE AUDIENCE AS S CONTINUES TO SPEAK.

S : I want to add one last comment and quote, which is actually the last footnote to the essay, as well as the last piece of text on the last page in 'God's Amateur' ... and it may as well serve also as the epilogue to these evenings and this issue. So now I'm quoting myself, then quoting myself quoting Large:
  "Large's approach falls in line with most of the other writers published by Hyphen Press. There are brief, enigmatic allusions to his novels in the books, notes and correspondence of Norman Potter and Anthony Froshaug, for example, which I like to imagine were deliberate acts of clue-planting for future close readers. Like Large, these writers work by simultaneous elucidation and example to articulate ideas which are the contents of the package represented by the label 'modernism'; contents implied by this last excerpt from 'Sugar in the Air' which refers to another fleeting critical spirit, the shadowy 'Muller', who—tellingly— disappears from the opening pages of the novel as soon as his point has been made:

When Muller quietly demonstrated that there are no 'Laws' in nature, that 'Facts' are only notions widely accepted, and that the subject matters of religion and philosophy are things more real than concrete and chrome steel, Pry was greatly shocked and surprised. When Muller went on to the subject of 'Values' Pry found that those things which he had come to regard as his ideals were falling about his head in a litter of unimportance, and his whole attitude to 'Life' stood revealed to him as trumpery, adolescent and mean. For this he blamed his social environment —until Muller went on to talk about 'Environment'.

And to REALLY end, a few words from our sponsors. As you may know, DOT DOT DOT has a very particular system of selling adverts, usually by fixing the rates of standard typeset pages according to the relative contrast between the page's type and its greyscale contrast. As everything in the issue must first be delivered in this room, vocally speaking, we're going to read the eight adverts according to the relative volume each has paid for.

THE ENDLESSLY RISING CANON STARTS AGAIN AND PLAYS THROUGHOUT THE REMAINING PAGES, ALTERNATELY READ BY D AND S AT APPROPRIATE VOLUMES.

HUDDLED IN ANIMATED CONVERSATION AROUND THE ROOM, A SIMILAR THOUGHT CROSSES THE MIND OF EACH MEMBER OF THE AUDIENCE: THE FIRST RULE IS ALWAYS PRODUCTION NEVER DOCUMENTATION; THE SECOND RULE IS THERE IS NO FIRST RULE. ∎

PROJECT NO.8

138 Division St.
New York, NY 10003
Tel: +1 212 925 5599
www.projectno8.com

1× Daily Before Meals, A Détacher, advice,
Alyssa Norton, angora brick, Anuschka
Hoevener, Arratia, Beer, badminton,
bags, bamboo, belt, bicycle, bison, Bless, black,
blue, books, Boudicca, Brian Janusiak, Chester
Wallace, Christian Marc Schmidt, Christian
Winjants, clogs, Creative Playthings, Daniel
Birnbaum, Daniel Chew, Danielle Aubert,
Dieter Rams, dresses, Elizabeth Beer, Excel
Drawings, Falke, flask, florescent, glass, gloves,
gold, green, Herbert Bayer, hippo tooth,
impala, Isa Genzken, jackets, Jan Tschichold,
Junghans, Katerina Seda, Kaweco, Kiosk,
Kostas Murkudis, L.G.R., laser-cutting,
leather, Liam Gillick, Lydia Rodrigues,
Maggie Trakas, Max Bill, men, mittens, music,
Natalia Brilli, necklaces, Niggli, Nuala, Obama,
Orla, Patrick Long, Paul Rand, pens, pin, pink,
plaid, Pyrex, radiant floor, red, rings, Roma,
Rootless Cosmopolitan, RSVP, Salvor, Seth
Kinmont, Schiesser, shirts, shorts, slippers,
socks, springbok, Stand By, Stephan Schnieder,
Stephanie Schneider, Sternberg Press,
still, t-shirts, Tom Scott, Tsurukichi, trousers,
turquoise, underwear, Various Projects,
Village, wallets, weather, wine, women,
wool, wristwatch, yellow.

WHERE'S MY FUCKING JET PACK?

Masters in Media Design.

The graduate Media Design Program turns ambitious thinkers and makers into leading designers within emerging communication contexts.

Application Deadline: February 1, 2009.
www.artcenter.edu/mdp

Graduate Media Design Program
Art Center College of Design
1700 Lida Street
Pasadena, CA 91103
+1 626 396-2469
mdpinfo@artcenter.edu

HYPHEN PRESS

"The winter is breaking up; the sun has passed the equinox, and there it is now, above me in the blue hemisphere, in magnificent combat with the clouds. It penetrates their fringes with a glorious radiance, angrily and insistently they drift past it in their masses, striving for domination of the sky. The earth is dark, the wind is cold and charged with snow. The clouds disperse, they tear apart and once again the sun bursts through, its radiant warmth instantly penetrates the cold air, an area of light moves over the tilled fields. Once again I am walking alone in the first days of spring. Whilst my friends engage in disputation and there is carnage in Spain, I shall walk from Ely to Colchester." ('The Stour Valley', 1937)

We have recently published two novels by E.C. Large: SUGAR IN THE AIR and ASLEEP IN THE AFTERNOON. Accompanying them is a third book, GOD'S AMATEUR: THE WRITING OF E.C. LARGE edited by Stuart Bailey and Robin Kinross, which republishes a selection of Large's short writings, including 'The Stour Valley'

Due in 2009 are books by O.F. Bollnow, Marie Neurath and Robin Kinross, plus TYPOGRAPHY PAPERS 8

www.hyphenpress.co.uk

STAND UP COMEDY

811 E. Burnside Street, Suite 111
Portland, Oregon 97214
t: +1 503.233.3382
f: +1 503.232.0200
info@shopstandingup.us
www.shopstandingup.us

When you're feeling sad and lonely, try some
stand up. It's so hard you'll feel instantly better
that it's not your profession. It is also often
necessary for Stand Up to simultaneously
assume the roles of writer, editor, performer,
promoter, producer, and technician. The next
time you're in town and in need of cheer,
redeem this for 20% off our goods.

NICE & FIT
WINTER 2008–9

November–December: Frederic D with
Fubbi Karlsson, PORTRAITS OFFICIELS

December: Inauguration of bookstore featuring
Dexter Sinister

January–February: OUR GREAT SHOW
Selections from the Jefferson Godard Collection

NICE & FIT
Brunnenstrasse 13
10119 Berlin
+49 30 440 45970
mail@niceandfitgallery.com
www.niceandfitgallery.com

CASCO ISSUES 11:
AN AMBIGUOUS CASE

Edited by: Emily Pethick, Marina Vishmidt
and Tanja Widmann

Contributions by: Babak Afrassiabi &
Nasrin Tabatabai (PAGES), Gregory Bateson,
Gregg Bordowitz, Judith Hopf, Jutta Koether,
Runo Lagomarsino, Kobe Matthys,
Metahaven, The Otolith Group, Emily Pethick,
Marina Vishmidt, Tanja Widmann

Designed by: Julia Born & Laurenz Brunner

Published by: Casco, Office for Art, Design
& Theory / Episode publishers

ISBN: 978-90-5973-108-0

Orders froMAN: info@cascoprojects.org /
info@episode-publishers.nl

Casco, Office for Art, Design and Theory
Nieuwekade 213-215
3511 RW, Utrecht
The Netherlands
www.cascoprojects.org
info@cascoprojects.org

WWW.LINETO.COM

DOT DOT DOT 17
Winter 2008/9
ISBN-13: 978-0-9794654-1-3

Published twice a year
by Dexter Sinister
38 Ludlow Street (Basement)
New York, NY 10002
U.S.A.
www.dextersinister.org
info@dextersinister.org

www.dot-dot-dot.us

EDITOR
Stuart Bailey
sinister@o-r-g.com
Los Angeles

This issue co-edited with
David Reinfurt
reinfurt@o-r-g.com
New York

Production/Coordination:
Sarah Crowner
sarah@dextersinister.org

THANKS
Claire Catterall
Andy Cooke
Maria Fusco
Frieze magazine
Jules Griffith
Anthony Huberman
Donna Huddleston
Robin Kinross
Sarah Mann
David Noonan
Genesis Breyer P-Orridge
Falke Pisano
Posy Simmonds
Maki Suzuki
Sue Thompson
Sara Le Turcq
Johnny Vivash
Thea Westreich / T.W.A.A.S.

PRINTING
Logotipas, Vilnius, Lithuania

All pieces translated by
editors/authors except
'The Middle of Nowhere'
by Will Holder.

CONTRIBUTORS

Agency
Brussels

Mark Beasley
New York

Stephen Beasley
London

Walead Beshty
Los Angeles

Dan Fox
London

James Goggin
London

Jörg Heiser
Berlin

Jennifer Higgie
London

Will Holder
London

Richard Hollis
London

Janice Kerbel
London

Alex Klein
Los Angeles

Malcolm McLaren
New York

Radim Peško
Amsterdam

Mike Sperlinger
London

Stefan Themerson
1920–1988

Erik van Zuylen
Amsterdam

DISPERSION

DDD is available
foremost from our own
point of distribution:
Dexter Sinister
Just-In-Time Workshop
& Occasional Bookstore
38 Ludlow Street (Basement)
New York, NY 10002
U.S.A.
OPEN SATURDAYS FROM
12 TO 6 PM
www.dextersinister.org
info@dextersinister.org

SUBSCRIPTIONS
1 year (2 issues):
€30 in Europe
$56 everywhere else
(worldwide exchange rates
subject to change) from:
Bruil & Van de Staaij
Postbus 75,
7940 AB Meppel
The Netherlands
T: +31 522 261 303
F: +31 522 257 827
info@bruil.info
www.bruil.info

DISTRIBUTION EUROPE
Coen Sligting Bookimport
Van Oldenbarneveldtstraat 77
1052 JW Amsterdam
The Netherlands
T: +31 20 673 2280
F: +31 20 664 0047
sligting@xs4all.nl

DISTRIBUTION UK
Central Books
115 Wallis Road
London E9 5LN
U.K.
T: +44 (0)845 458 9911
F: +44 (0)845 458 9912
orders@centralbooks.com
www.centralbooks.com

DISTRIBUTION AMERICAS,
ASIA, AFRICA, AUSTRALIA
Princeton Architectural Press
37 E 7th Street
New York, NY 10003
U.S.A.
T: +1 212 995 9620
F: +1 212 995 9454
sales@papress.com
www.papress.com

ADVERTISING
DDD adverts are paid
according to the background
greyscale percentage;
contact <sarah@dextersinister.
org> for rates or reservations

STOP PRESS

THE FORM OF THE BOOK
A one-day conference on
book design

St Bride Library
Friday 30 January 2009
9.30am–6pm

'The Form of the Book' brings
together highly acclaimed
graphic designers, design
critics and design historians
to discuss various aspects
of book design. Themes such
as materiality, typographic
detailing, design historiogra-
phy, artist's books, methods
of production and design
ideology run throughout
the day, in an exciting line-up
of international speakers.
With Chrissie Charlton,
Jenny Eneqvist/Roland Früh/
Corina Neuenschwander,
James Goggin, Sarah Gottlieb,
Richard Hollis, Mevis &
Van Deursen and Catherine
de Smet.

Curated by Sara De Bondt
and Fraser Muggeridge.

Full rate: £60/£50 Friends
of St Bride Library.
Students & over 60s: £30/£25
Friends of St Bride Library

Book at www.stbride.org
or call 0207 353 3331

St Bride Library
Bride Lane, Fleet Street
London EC4 Y8EE
www.stbride.org

GAZE FIXEDLY INTO

CRYSTAL's

FORSEEING EYE

And A Peaceful **STILLNESS** Befalls You, A Gentle Flowing **CALM** Of The Kind Induced By **PSYCHOTROPICS** Alone — All

That Surrounds You Fades To A **SOUNDLESS HAZE** As **UNWANTED THOUGHTS** Dissolve Into Vapour — **TIME** Rushes Past Like

A Leaf On The Wind — LIMBS SOFTEN, COLOURS MERGE, MINDS OPEN And

HIDDEN TRUTHS, DISTANT FUTURES

COME TO LIGHT IN THE

CLOUDY GLOW OF HER MONOCULAR STARE.

Look No Further

RICHES! TRAVELS! PASSION! HEALTH! HEARTACHE!

DECEPTION! HARDSHIP! DESPAIR!

In The SINGULAR FOCUS OF HER GUIDING WHITE ORB

(clearing the air of negative vibrations and electromagnetic toxins),

FAR BECOMES NEAR AND THEN BECOMES NOW.

Vague Random Images Yield Dazzling CLARITY — specific & general, casual & solemn, urgent & fanciful —,

Revealing Your Fate, Seeing You Bravely On Your Way.

– BUT WAIT! –

Like A Lizard To A Rock, Like The Sun To The Moon, Like A Fugitive To The Night,

BELIEVE WHAT YOU SEE BUT BLINK AND YOU'LL MISS

Not the **BIGGEST**, Not the **TALLEST**, Not the **SMARTEST**, Not the **STRONGEST**; Not the **SMALLEST**, Not the **SHORTEST**, Not

the **DUMBEST**, Not the **WEAKEST**,

BASHFUL FROM BIRTH

HUMBLER THAN BOILED CROW. The Most Modest, Most Elusive, Most Confounding and Inconspicuous,

IN THE VERY CORNER OF YOUR EYE

catch a fleeting glimpse of

THE SHYEST PERSON ALIVE

BLINDSPOT.

MASTERFULLY ECLIPSING YOUR GLANCE

WITHOUT EVER SHOWING HER FULL CRYPTIC SELF

(unexplained by psychology, metaphysics, religion or the occult; neither transparent, reflective, patterned or subterranean)

The **QUICK SILKY** Moves Of This **PERIPHERAL PRESENCE**

WILL DEFTLY DEFY THE MOST

VISUALLY ASTUTE.